FROM THE Spotlight TO HIS GLORIOUS Light

Durstola

The EC Publishing LLC books may be ordered
through booksellers or by contacting:

EC Publishing LLC
116 South Magnolia Ave.
Suite 3, Unit F
Ocala, FL 34471, USA
Direct Line: +1 (352) 644-6538
Fax: +1 (800) 483-1813
http://www.ecpublishingllc.com/

Ordering Information:
Quantity sales. Special discounts are available on quan-
tity purchases by corporations, associations, and others.
For details, contact the publisher at the address above.

Printed in the United States of America

Table of Contents

Acknowledgements

I am so grateful to God for Abraham; the husband He chose for me. Abraham gives me so much supporting love. He built in me the foundation that caused me to believe I can write books in English. This one is "My Memories" of a lifetime learning.

My deep thanks to our friend Peter Lazar, who stands beside us and who has labored to complete this book project and insert pictures.

Dedication

This book of my "Memories" is dedicated to my three children.
Esther, Eric and Nouchka. To know more, who their parents are.

BECAUSE WHAT YOU ARE WILLING TO CONFRONT
GOD IS WILLING TO HEAL. (P. White)

FROM THE SPOTLIGHT TO HIS GLORIOUS LIGHT

Foreword

A Wise man once said:
"Hate has 4 letters but so does Love.
Enemy has 7 letters but so does Friends.
Lying has 5 letters but so does Truth.
Cry has 3 letters but so does Joy.
Negativity has 10 letters but so does Positivity.
LIFE IS 2 SIDED, SO CHOOSE THE BETTER SIDE OF IT."
(Shehzad Ahmadw)

My daughter says to me; "Mom, you must write your story! The whole truth of your life in show business and why you did a "U turn" faith Journey and I will redact it for you. It will resonate in the hearts of those going through similar situations and bring about healing through faith."

THE LORD SAYS, "I WILL RESCUE THOSE WHO LOVE ME. I WILL BE WITH THEM IN TROUBLE. I WILL RESCUE THEM AND HONOR THEM."

Yes! Nouchka I will; TELL THE TRUTH THE WHOLE TRUTH AND NOTHING BUT THE TRUTH!

Chapter 1

THE BELT OF TRUTH

A few years ago, I had a dream, which made a big impact in my way of thinking and talking. In my dream, I was dancing on my toe shoes, in front of Jesus my Lord.

He was sitting on the throne, covered in light. I danced with all my strength. Jumping, flying. I was amazing! Of course! it was a dream...

I finished on my knees before the Lord.

When I looked up, Jesus was smiling. Then he gestured to two angels to tell them to bring something to me. My heart pounding with joy, I received from them a magnificent gold belt, covered with precious stones. I was in ecstasy... but when they put the belt on me, the weight was too much for my tiny body. I could hardly move.

I said; "Lord it's so beautiful! But it is too heavy for me, I cannot dance with it."

The Lord said; "I know it's heavy, it is the BELT OF TRUTH, and you need to wear it every day of your life!"

I awoke with this feeling of this enormous belt around my waist. I never forgot that dream.

To write my story, is difficult to write about myself without bragging, because to be in show business, you must be a show off, to be noticed, and fame was my goal.

My picture was on the front page of the newspaper in Italy, 1962.

Mimi Desly all'Open Gate

Continua il successo dei castigatissimi « Paul Steffen Dancers » all'« Open Gate ». Mimì Desly, una bella ragazza bionda che fa parte del balletto si è fatta ammirare per la sua esuberanza. Presto la vedremo in televisione: spera di essere uno dei principali numeri di attrazione dell'ormai noto balletto. Auguri

I was, in those days, number one, ballerina and choreographer.
The best of the worst, ha! Ha! ha.

My stage life was more important to me than love, money and yes God. My prayers were always "God help me to have more success than those who performed before me."

I would read the Bible and some scriptures would stay with me from the last book of Revelations.

REVELATION (21:6-8) "I AM THE ALPHA AND THE OMEGA THE BEGINNING AND THE END. I WILL GIVE OF THE FOUNTAIN OF THE WATER OF LIFE FREELY TO HIM WHO THIRSTS.

BUT THE FEARFUL, AND UNBELIEVING,

AND THE ABOMINABLE,

AND MURDERERS,

AND WHOREMONGERS,

AND SORCERERS,

AND IDOLATERS,

"AND ALL LIARS"

SHALL HAVE THEIR PART IN THE LAKE WHICH BURNS WITH FIRE AND BRIMSTONE WHICH IS THE SECOND DEATH."

From time to time, I would be elated in the spiritual, but for the most part, what I enjoyed most was admiration. I became more attracted by the spotlight than Jesus.

My beginning was not a cup of tea.

Becoming a prima ballerina did not come easy as I endured many health issues. I began ballet school when I was around 9 years old. At age 13, I got Meningitis with Poliomyelitis virus followed by partial paralysis in my left side. For months my mother took me to the Municipal pool. That was my physical therapy. After a year, I became a competing swimmer in the National team.

Two years later, I was back in ballet school and my Russian teacher, Professor Cheloudiakoff, always encouraged me to go to audition for the theatre.

He would say: "You have good elevation, do your specialty and show your personality, be spectacular!"

I took his advice and was immediately accepted with a full scholarship. I said good bye to my family to begin my internship in the ballet school for the preparation of "LES PETITS RATS DE L'OPERA" miles away from home. That was tough!

An Operetta company was looking for ballerinas who could sing and talk on stage for a twelve months contract in Switzerland with nice pay plus boarding.

I thought, wow to be paid to do what I love? (My favorites movies to watch were with, Fred Astaire, Gene Kelly and Cyd Charisse!) That was my dream.

I auditioned and was accepted.

The first night in Switzerland, the theatre was packed, the owner of the company, Jeany Walker, was the star of the show. She was an opera singer.

She took center stage on a pedestal in a beautiful long gown, singing.

We, the ballerinas, wore long tutus in different colors and we dance around the opera singer 3 times on the right and then 3 times on the left. I followed instructions the first round, but then something happened without much thought process. I decided to incorporate something more uplifting, so when the other ballerinas were dancing on the right, I went to the left, causing chaotic interaction in each direction. The audience started laughing which encouraged me to do more. I continued and pretended to fall grabbing another girl, pulling down her tutu. People were cracking up and all the ballerinas started laughing. Jeany Walker lost her voice as everyone's laughter took over.

When the show was over, Jeany Walker and the director of the theatre called me in for a meeting.

The others were whispering to each other saying I was going to get fired.

Jeany Walker was furious, she asked: What happened!? Do you have stage fright for acting like that?"

I answered her; "No, I just wanted to be noticed.

She was mad, now yelling; "Yes you are noticed!!! For acting the fool!"

The director of the theater just arrived to the meeting with a big smile.

He said; "That was the best show we had in a long time! that is exactly what we need, you made people happy, please don't change anything."

Jeany Walker was perplexed, but the contract was important to her, and so she accepted to give me more of a leading role. After a year, the company returned to France.

I had just turned 19 and stayed in Switzerland with another girl who decided to stay there as she fell in love with a lawyer.

Doctor Delgrande was also a regular visitor to the theatre. He was well known for his radical new treatments and his humorist personality. Everyone wanted to be in his entourage and I felt privileged to be one of his guests, often invited to his lavish home. He was a bachelor in his 40's or 50's, not much of a looker but what a fantastic personality! We became good friends pretty quick. We enjoyed each other's company as we could talk about the arts, and we both have a good sense of humor.

He told me a story when he took me to visit my family in France 400 km away in his sports car, which only took about 4 hours at the speed we were going.

He had a way with telling stories that really pulled you in, as if you were there in the midst of it all.

He lit a cigarette and began telling it.

"One day a desperate man came to beg me to save his wife who was dying in one of the best hospitals of the country. All different types of specialists trying everything but none were able to heal her. Her health was deteriorating fast.

The man said; "Please Doctor, I will pay you anything if you can just save my wife, I love her. She is my life!"

I did a case study on everything that was done to her, and did exactly the opposite that all the specialists had done, and saved her life.

I sent him the bill.

The man was furious and took me to court. I showed up to court without a lawyer to defend myself. The court room was full. After the defendant exposed the case.

The Judge asked; "Doctor Delgrande, can you tell the court how this exuberant bill is justified?"

In which I replied, yes, of course your honor, this man came to me saying he would pay anything to save his wife, in which I delivered exactly that.

Then I turned to face the man who was sitting with his wife holding her hand.

I asked him; "Do you think your wife's life is worth less than that?"

The wife looked at her husband. The husband was a very rich man. He blushes, then he stood up and bowed. Then paid the bill."

Chapter 2

GENEVA

Jim one of the male singers and me, decided to go to Geneva.

When we got there, we received the bad news. The theatre had burned down and was in restoration mode. To save money, we took one modest hotel room to share. We contacted a talent agency and the only work option was a night club. The pay for one night with two shows was paid better than an entire week in a company and it included a studio apartment.

But that was not ballet. I needed to do two dances. I made two new costumes and chose the music, "An American in Paris" and "Moonlight serenade". I worked on the choreography but with a totally different genre, that was Jazz! One with red tutu on ballet toes shoes.

Jim did not get the job; he was going back to Paris that was our last day together. Jim had always teased me because I was a virgin at 19 years old. He was shaving.

He says to me; "I have news for you! You are not a virgin anymore Mimi I took your virginity when you were sleeping."

I screamed!!! I thought I was going to die I trusted him. I thought he was my friend.

My virginity was reserved only for the man I was going to marry morality was engraved in my heart the way I was taught in my family and now I was a disgrace. I grabbed all my belonging and rushed out.

Jim was laughing, shouting; "I married you!!!"

I was crying, walking in the street, I did not know what to do. I can never go back home. I finally calmed down and went to rehearse my new dance with the orchestra.

I needed to be there by 10 pm to meet everybody.

I got there and sat at the bar waiting to perform on stage and checking out the orchestra which was surprisingly very good. People were eating and drinking. I noticed I was the youngest one there. Women were wearing nice long evening gowns. I was wearing a nice modest short white dress near the neckline, contrasting to deep lowcut neckline of the hostess around the bar.

One of the hostesses tells me "I' will give you 5 Francs if you have this American guy at the end of the bar buy you a drink."

I asked "Why?"

She said "We all tried but he pushed us away."

5 Suisse Francs, in those years could buy food for a week. Of course I will try. I went to sit behind him. I pretended to fall from the stool pushing him and fell on top of his foot.

I apologized. He looked at me from my feet, (wearing flat ballerina shoes) all the way to my head.

He said; "What the hell are you doing here? you should be in bed you're just a baby!"

Reluctantly, I answered; "I am not a baby, I am 19 years old, and I am dancing in the show tonight" Whispering, I continued. This lady at the other side of the bar will give me 5 Francs if you buy me a drink."

He started laughing and ordered champagne.

After the two shows, Russell introduced himself and I told him my name was Mimi. He asked me to go with him to eat at the train station, the only place where the restaurant stayed open late.

When we arrived in his beautiful new Mercedes, the restaurant was closed.

Mercedes 1959

That was the first time in my life I was sitting in this luxurious new model Mercedes. These were rare in the 50's. Sitting in the passenger seat, I asked him where he got this car. He said he ordered it by phone from London to the factory in Germany, after 6 months he just went to pick it up. He said; "The car comes with a 20 years warranty. If anything happens anywhere you are, they will send a Mercedes specialist mechanic in less than 24 hours."

Russell was speaking in French with a delightful American accent. He said he was hungry I told him I have crackers and a can of sardines at my place.

He said; "let's go."

After eating, Russell was sitting in the only big arm chair, asking; "Can I stay here until 8 am? I don't have a hotel reservation and it is very late."

My answer was; "Of course you can sleep in that chair."

I went to the bathroom to put on my dignified warm blue satin pajamas, and went into my bed. And I fell asleep immediately.

I woke up feeling that something was coming into my bed. I put my hand under my pillow, took my revolver and put it at Russell's head. I told him to get out of my place. He jumped out, put on his trousers and disappeared. I locked the door and went back to sleep.

In the afternoon, the noise of a horn woke me up. I looked through the window, and there was the Mercedes parked outside with Russell asking me to go to a restaurant with him. I liked that very much, but in France if someone invites you, to be polite you refuse and if the person insists that means they really want to invite you.

I refused and Russell got in his car and drove away! What? No second invite? Shoot!! I did not think that would happen.

Russell was American and I learned to never refuse the first invitation from an American again.

The following night, I showed up to work and surprise! Russell was there waiting for me. At the end of the night, he invited me to go to a well-known upscale restaurant the following evening. He said he will pick me up at a certain time and asked if I have a watch. I told him I never possessed a watch.

The next day, he picked me up earlier than planned, took me to a jewelry store and told me to choose a watch. There were so many beautiful watches to choose from. Some with diamonds and gold. After I looked at all the options, I spotted a small watch with a leather band.

I said; "That one is nice"

He lowered his head and said "Are you sure?"

It was probably the least expansive one. Maybe it was a test, to see what kind of person I was.

Then he said; "If you have a good family, why are you working in a night club?"

I wore my hair in a pony tail, tight black pants, white shirt with a skinny black tie and black ballerina shoes. I really did look like a teenager. Russell was 39, a captain instructor pilot for Pan American.

He was handsome, tall with hazelnut eyes. He wore a tailored suit and was well mannered, pulling the chair for me to sit, opening the car door, sitting only after I sat. He treated me like a lady. He insisted to take me back home to my parents. I refused.

Russell went to talk to the owner of the night club, threatening him to let me go. I was not happy about Russell acting like a father, but I had no other choice.

Chapter 3

SENSATIONAL ENTRANCE

I felt the peering eyes of the people looking at us driving into my neighborhood. Russell parks the car in front of my house as the people stare to get a glimpse at who would own a luxurious car like that. They probably thought we were famous. My parents were very thankful to Russell for bringing me back home and wanted to show the appreciation with a feast.

Russell liked my little town. He respectfully went to stay at a local hotel on the same street. The next day, he invited us, my parents and my younger brother, in a fancy restaurant a few miles away. The town welcomed him, honoring Americans who came to liberate us in WWII.

I was born in France during WWII in a cave (cellar in English) during the Nazi occupation, at my grandmother's home. A nice neighborhood that the Nazis occupied just across my grandmother's house. This was their head quarter where they arrested and tortured French people.

Some scenes are carved in my memories... I remember at around 3 years old, watching my mother, her two younger sisters and grandmother praying and putting their hands tight over their ears to stop hearing the screaming from across the street.

Being Alsatians, my parents were fluent in French and German.

My mother was arrested. Someone had exposed her being the wife of my father who was part of "La Resistance", a group that fought against the Nazi occupation in France during the war.

(My Mother with my sister and me)

My Father was a "Maquisard." The Maquis were rural guerrilla bands of French Resistance fighters.

The war started just after the last National Gymnastics Championship, where my father won with his team.

As soon the war started my father went right away in the special commando in the L I S Sabotage Operation Services inter Allie Mission.

My grandmother was night and day on her knees, interceding for my mom's safety. She and my two aunts were taking care of me and my older sister who was traumatized from the drastic changes the war brought on. She was born 2 years before the war, and for her it was very hard to adapt, unlike me who was accustomed to what I had only experienced being born in this situation.

My mom returned and was forced to open the barber shop, for the German army. She had never cut anyone's hair. My dad was the barber and before she married my father, she worked in a hospital as a nurse. Trembling and shaking, she proceeded to shaving and cutting hair. One young Nazi officer insisted for a bottle of cologne. My mother told him everything was gone. The officer took his pistol and put it against my mother's head. An older officer who was waiting for his turn stood up, asking the young officer to go outside to talk. I don't know if the older officer spared my mother's life because he needed a haircut or if that was yet another miracle.

The first 5 years of my life were lived most of the time in this cellar. Sometime I was carried in a hurry through the underground tunnel of the Historic Castle near our home, as soon as the bombing sirens started.

Emma, who was our nearest neighbor, always grabbed me when the sirens started and my mother carried my sister. Emma was big breasted and she carried me tight against her chest, my head in the middle. It felt like two pillows muffling out the noise, and I could fall asleep peacefully in the midst of all the chaos.

The only food I remember was 1/2 a potato a day, cooked on charcoal in the cellar with a candle and of course, my mother's milk.

At the liberation the Americans came with cans of beans and other stuff. One American officer took me on his knee and gave me a little candy roll of many colors. I looked at it, but did not know what it was. The officer opened it and took out a little red thing with a hole in the middle and put it in my mouth. It was like a symphony of heavenly music in my mouth. Quite fitting for my first candy to be called "LIFE SAVERS".

Russell was for me a sweet memory of "LIVE SAVERS".

Russell was a Captain Fighter Pilot in the war against the Japanese when they came to attack PEARL HARBOR in 1941.

Russell came from an English family, his ancestors immigrated in America in the 1670's to escape Cromwell, who ruthlessly ruled England, in 1642.

I did not want to stay with my parents. I was freaking out that I did not have my period. I was three weeks late. I did not want to bring dishonor to my family. I wrote a note to my parents after everyone was asleep, that I needed to take my life because I was no longer a virgin, asking for their forgiveness. And swallowed every sleeping pill in the bottle.

Early, my mother discovered my note and called the doctor. She then immediately made me swallow salted coffee, and my father followed by slapping me and putting pressure on my stomach to make me vomit.

The doctor washed my stomach. The priest came to give me the last rites.

Russell arrived in the middle of the commotion. My mother said; "Mimi almost died!" But his French was not perfect, and he thought she said, "Mimi just died!". He rushed to the toilet to throw up. She followed him and explained to him what had happened.

After few days I confessed to my mother what happened with Jim.

My mother asked me: "That happened when you were sleeping? you must feel something".

I answered; "No nothing."

She and I were very embarrassed to talk about it. In those days people did not talk about sex, especially in a Christian family, it was out of place and vulgar.

Russell offered a solution to my parents. To take me to Bern, Switzerland, where abortion was legal as opposed to France, and he will take care of all the expenses.

Chapter 4

BERN

It would be 11 days until the appointment to see the doctor. Russell chose a first-class hotel. I could not believe how luxurious the place was. The hotel room was quite large with two Queen-size beds on each bed was a big gold medallion with the emblems of the city of Bern, two bears.

Russell says to me "open it" inside the round gold metallic paper was Swiss chocolate.

The enormous bathroom took my breath away, with two white bathrobes and slippers. I forgot for a moment my condition.

In the days that followed, Russell decided to give me a new wardrobe, as to look more like a classy lady and less like a teenager. He had me modelling the outfits. First a navy- blue satin dress, then a brown silk dress and then a 3 pieces suit color purple-eggplant, that looked stunning with a 10 strings pearl necklace, and of course, Bally high heeled shoes.

We enjoyed going around town to theaters, restaurants, museums, art galleries, vernissage and cocktail parties.

One morning, I woke up feeling something was leaking out of me. I thought it was urine so I rushed to the bathroom but it was blood. Alarmed, I called Russell to take me to the hospital. Russell started to ask me questions, I told him my story with Jim.

Russell said; "If that was the first time you have sex, for sure you would wake up. You are fine that is your period, the guy was Joking. Stress sometimes can stop your period you are a virgin."

Jim's stupid joke almost cost me my life and a lot of pain to my parents.

On the other hand, I was happy to be experiencing all these amazing things with Russell. He was for me like the professor in "My Fair Lady", always teaching me about art, famous painters and writers.

Can you imagine an American, teaching a French girl to have class? I admired and respected him. Up until that point, being a show girl was the most important thing in my life. Russell was surprised to find out how innocent and naive I was.

My mother never explained anything to me about sex and my parents never walked in their underwear in front of us. They were always decently dressed.

My mother made herself up every day early in the morning prior to us seeing her. Hair, make-up and always with nice dresses. She told me, when you get married, you must always look your best, that will make your husband feel that you care about him. Only people in their pajamas all day where sick people.

The first time Russell kissed me, was in the car, coming out of a night club... and I completely melted in his arms.

From that day on, Russell became the most important person in the whole world to me.

He rescued me expecting nothing. He was all mine, I belonged to him, and he was, like the "Life Savers", my first love.

I told him "Now you are my husband"

He said; "I am 20 years older than you, one day you are going to leave me for a guy your age. But I keep you until then, what you love is not me, but the Mercedes and all those new things."

I told him; "One day I will buy a better car than yours, one like the Queen from England, just wait and watch!"

Russell was laughing and said "That is what I like about you; you are adventurous, and very funny."

I used to make him laugh; doing an exaggerated impersonation of the people we watched in the theatre and people we met.

Life with Russell was full of surprises. One evening we went to see a very good Jazz Orchestra in a night club. Russell was drinking more than one scotch, and I stayed with one glass of champagne for the entire night.

Russell said; "We have nothing in common, you don't smoke, you don't drink."

He took me by the hand and started to dance and sing to me, like Gene Kelly. I felt like I was in a fairy tale, he then stopped and asked the trumpet player to lend his instrument. With the ok, he jumped on the stage and started to play the trumpet like a pro. Just like Louis Armstrong. Everybody stopped dancing, watching in amazement! He got a standing ovation. I was so proud to be with such a talented man. Russell also played the piano.

He loved music but his passion was painting. Russell asked me to be his model, he sketched me in every angle. One day he spontaneously announced we should go to Cannes on the French Riviera.

There he rented a big beautiful villa to be able to paint.

In the local cafeteria we met with other artists, both painters and writers. We made many friends that were fond of us.

One day Russell gave me the keys to the Mercedes.

He said; "I cannot stop to paint, please go buy some cigarettes and something for dinner."

I looked at him surprised and said; "I have never driven a car alone by myself!"

Russell responded; "You can do it you can do anything if you want to. I flew a plane when I was 14 years old, because I wanted to. Just watch out for the traffic."

Wow! I am driving the Mercedes! In those days, it was a rarity for females to drive cars. After shopping, I passed near the "Cafeteria" where our friends were sitting out drinking coffee, they gestured for me to stop. I asked them if they would like to go to the next little town up the mountain, about 15 miles away.

Enthusiastically they shouted; "YES!"

It was a two-way narrow road, enough space for two cars, going up, on the right was the large rocks and on the left was the cliff. I was so proud to show off, I was driving at a fast speed passing every car.

One of the two guys said; "Don't you think you are going too fast? passing all those cars, on those turns, you cannot see the other vehicles coming from the opposite way. When did you get your driver's license?"

I answered; "I don't have a driving license!"

They both exclaimed simultaneously; "WHAT?!"

The older one asked; "When did you start to drive this car?"

I responded; "Today is my first time."

They screamed; "STOP!! Stop the car! We don't want to die!"

I stopped the car and told them it is a long way back to the town. They insisted they preferred to walk.

I smiled all the way driving back home, the gate was open, just enough space for a car to go in. I had to go carefully and slowly, but instead of putting my foot on the brake, I made a mistake and put my foot on the accelerator and passed the gate speeding.

OUCH! But not one scratch.

Russell told me he was watching from the window and had to rush to take two aspirins.

Chapter 5

MADRID

After a few months, we went back to Geneva for the U.N convention. There, Russell met with some Spanish guys. One of them, named Romero, wanted to buy the Mercedes in exchange for some cash and a one year stay in his Madrid apartment.

Russell loved the idea to be able to study art in the Prado Museum.

Back at the hotel, he says; "Change of plan, pack up, we are going to Madrid today."

The Madrid apartment was a large penthouse, the terrace was very spacious but being on the top floor we had problems with the central heater. The maintenance personnel showed Russell what to do to make it work better, just to unscrew the valve to let the air get out, until the hot water comes out and then screw it back on. But not to touch the others, only that one.

One day Russell was yelling; "Mime come fast with a big pot!"

I run to the bedroom with the biggest pot I could find, not knowing what it was for. The scene was catastrophic or hilarious depending on the mood!

Russell, the bed and the wall, all covered with dirty water. Russell thought he could make the heater in the bedroom work better if he just unscrewed it, and do the same like the one in the living room, but he was not supposed to do that, the hot water pressure was so strong that it blew the screw out. He was trying to stop the water and to put the screw back and burning his fingers in the process. I told him I was going to call the maintenance guy but Russell was too proud to accept help for the mess he did, and insisted he would be able to fix it himself. He did it. But what a big mess!

One day, I was cooking a lamb leg, I cut a small piece to test if it was done, the morsel got stuck in my throat, I tried to cough but I was chocking. Painfully, I walked to Russell's studio at the end of the hall, opened the door, and gestured to him and then collapsed. He understood immediately, he first tried the emergency Heimlich, but it did not work. He then grabbed one of my legs with one hand, lifted me upside down and with the other hand he gave me a series of back blows, and the piece of meat went out. After that he held me in his arms. He saved my life.

What a stupid way to die, he said. We laughed.

It was a beautiful day, to have a nice date in via San Jose Antonio, one of Madrid's most elegant streets. After having a delicious lunch at 'AL Manila', Russell took me to a beauty salon, and told the owner to make me look like his wife instead of his daughter, because the parents of Romero came to visit and thought I was Russell's daughter.

I got a beautiful silver blue color hairstyle, my long hair nicely rolled up on the top of my head, plus light make up. Now I looked more like 25 years old instead of 16, with a nice suit and high heels.

I loved the way I looked. Like we say in French "L'habit fait le Moine". Literal translation means "the clothes make the monk." And yes, I now looked the part of this man's wife.

Two years later, we went back to Geneva. We enjoyed Switzerland because everything was so clean, and the furnished apartments was always with a delightful luxurious style.

All the restaurants were so much better than the other European cities.

One year later, Russell was up early, he says he needed to go out to buy cigarettes. Late at night he was not back, I started to worry that something happened to him, lately he was drinking more and more. He left me just a little cash not enough to pay the rent which was coming up. I always kept my ballet shoes and did ballet routine exercises. I called an agent and asked if I could have an immediate contract. He says I can start the same night at a club called, "La Cave a Bob".

A week later, Russell came back. He was very disappointed to see me going back to dance in night clubs. I told him he did not give me another choice, and where was he? He said, the day he went to buy cigarettes he had breakfast at the airport and found one of his friend's, a pilot, there eating. They had a good time together drinking, then went to the sauna to sober up. Then he flew with him to London, where Russell's ex-wife and daughter lives and he got back today. Just like that!

I told him I cannot depend on him anymore. He must accept that I have the right to provide for my needs. Reluctantly he agreed.

I signed contracts for Belgium, Holland, Germany, Italy and Switzerland. Traveling alone most of the time. Russell would come to visit me for a week or so every month.

In 1962 I bought a Daimler Regency, the same car as the Queen mother of England, with my own money that I made in show business and doing movies in Milano with Fernando Garcia ballet.

Daimler 1962

I realized Russell became an alcoholic. He tried a few times to stop, but always went back. He had a studio for himself to paint. He was very good and started to have exhibitions of his paintings. He was mainly doing portraits. He did a nice big poster for me when I started to make a name for myself with innovative choreography and Parodies.

After 7 years of living together, I became pregnant. I was back in Switzerland to do my last contract in the Moulin Rouge in Geneva, with an outstanding orchestra and a stage made of glass with lights underneath, which gave it an amazing spotlight effect. I performed two times every night until I was 7 months pregnant.

The only food I was able to eat and not vomit was steamed foods, butter milk and carrot juice.

Russell insisted for me to take multi vitamins for pregnant women. My weight was a solid 115 pounds, (instead of my usual 102 pounds). I put on the extra 13 pounds throughout my pregnancy. I had to wear a girdle under my light pink leotard and wore long transparent dresses with crystals and glitter. All the spotlights on my costumes giving a magical effect, dancing on toe shoes, no one suspected that I was pregnant.

The director of the Moulin Rouge came to me after my last show.

He said; "Mimi, here sign this, we like your show and we want you to come back in June."

I answered; "Thank you but I can't I am going to have a baby!"

He started to laugh at me, and continued; "First you need to get pregnant, until then you can sign this contract."

I said; "But I am 7 months pregnant, I am expecting in April."

An expression of surprise on his face, he asked; "But where is your baby belly? And how can you dance on your toes?"

I lifted up my dress and showed him the girdle and said; "Why do you think I changed all my costumes with these long floating veils and had new choreography, eliminating big jumps and using more light effects."

Russell insisting on us to get married.

I told him; "What kind of marriage will that be? You drink, are two times divorced before me and we cannot have a marriage in the church anyway."

His answer was; "We need to go to City Hall to be legally married for the sake of the baby, not to be born illegitimate."

We had our permanent rental home in Bern, many artists living in this building and two of them came to be our witnesses, between two shows.

This was not a dream wedding.

For the wedding, I wore a mini trapeze pink satin dress with pearls and my black Astrakhans fur coat with grey mink collar and hat.

After this, only the two of us, went right away back home. We ate a pink lobster salad that I made, no flowers no nothing. Then I slept.

During the night I started to be in labor but I waited until the morning to wake up Russell. He took me to an exclusive private Clinic.

In Europe Clinics are well known for advanced medical care as opposed to the local hospitals. The gynecologist prepared me. He was concerned because I did not have much water and my stomach had a belt of muscles blocking the passage. I was in labor for 22 hours. In those days, doctors will only do C. section in case of an emergency. I was rushed for an emergency C. section.

When I woke up, a nurse put in my arms the most beautiful baby girl in the whole world. Perfect little nose, perfect little mouth. She was absolutely perfect, but she had a tiny bandage on the left of her forehead. I asked why? The nurse explained her head was already engaged to come out when I was in labor but she was blocked by the belt of muscles so the doctor carefully made an incision when he opened me up, it was just a small scratch and would disappear soon.

Russell arrived with a beautiful pink elephant porcelain flower pot.

In 1967, the sex of the baby was not revealed until the birth and the way I carried, we thought we were having a boy and thought to call him Hall like his father's middle name, Russell Hall Hinman. But it was an adorable baby girl.

I was reading the story of Queen Esther in my Bible, who was the chosen one amongst all the beautiful girls. Yes! Esther was a perfect name.

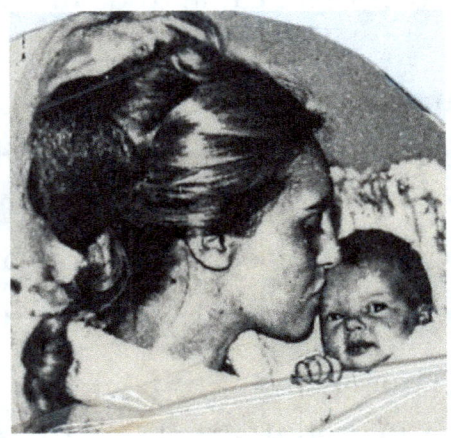

Esther became the most precious treasure of my life she captivated all my attention.

Russell told me to call my parents to let them know that we had a baby girl. I never told my parents I was pregnant. The last time we visited them Russell was drunk and made a big scandalous scene in the town. My father had told me to give up on him.

But I could not do that, he saved my life. When he was sober, he was the most morally respectable man.

I called my parents and they came to visit me in the hospital with gifts for the baby. Russell stayed away until they left. I told my parents that we got married, and the birth of Esther changed Russell's attitude and he stopped drinking.

After two weeks in the hospital and breastfeeding day and night, Baby Esther and I were healthy and ready to go home.

One month later we decided to go to the Aletsch glacier in the Switzerland mountains, at 2800 meters altitude.

Our friend let us use her cottage to live a primitive healthy lifestyle. The cabin was built by her father's own hands against the rocky mountain, about 75 years before. No electricity, no bathroom and we needed to pick wood and cook in a rock fireplace. Everything was like living 100 years in the past.

I was enthusiastic about this complete change of life. Russell thought it was crazy with a 40 days old baby, 2 hours away walking distance on the mountain just to reach the nearest phone at a tourist restaurant.

In 1967 cell phones did not exist. The water passage from the mountain came on a rock, next to the cabin from the melting ice, like a small waterfall.

One day, Russell was painting a nature scenery outside the cabin and in came a herd of cows from the valley. They claimed a spot right there where Russell was painting. He ran with his easel and paints in hand shouting;

"Take the baby inside! Those cows are like tanks destroying everything!"

Instead, I took off my long sleeve shirt, using my shirt like a cow-boy rope and I ran after the cows doing big arm movements with my shirt yelling "AY! AY! AY!" And the cows quickly ran away.

Russell looked at me with admiration, and said; "I can see you have farmer blood in your veins."

Coming from him, that was not a compliment! As he was a city boy. But the comment did bring back memories of wonderful vacations in my father's hometown, Seebach in Alsace, with all the charming folklore at my uncle's farm with my cousins, riding horses, taking the cows in the big pastures and climbing cherry trees.

Our Swiss cabin was the side of a doll house. Everything was handmade and small. The bunkbed was not big enough to sleep two, so I slept on the top with baby Esther glued to me like a stamp, and Russell slept on the bottom.

One night I woke up and saw Russell sitting at the tiny table with a candle looking at the door. I heard a continual knock at the door.

I asked; "What is it?"

He said; "It's a big toad"

I told him; "Just throw her out and go back to sleep"

He answered; "That thing is disgusting I cannot do that!"

I jumped out of the bed, picked up the toad by the legs, opened the small window and threw it out. Russell ceremoniously was bowing and shaking my hand.

In the end of July, Russell wanted us to go back to Bern, he had an appointment to meet with the owner of an art gallery. I insisted to stay in the cabin with Esther. I liked the solitude and the serenity of the place. Hesitating, he finally left.

We had friends, a couple, who lived on this mountain their entire life. Sina and Jose, her husband, who was a guide for the tourists. They lived down from us about a 25 minutes' walk. They had a farm with fresh milk and eggs.

They visited often to see if I needed anything. Esther was only on my milk, and now almost 4 months old, she needed some solid baby food. Doctor Bamatter a famous Swiss pediatrician, who was visiting every year the place where he was born, he found out that baby Esther was living there. And decided to come to visit us despite his old age with his 2 young nurses. He came and prayed a blessing over Esther. It was such a beautiful time together.

The nearest town was 3 hours away, but to catch the cable car on the top of the mountain, I needed to walk up to the top which took about 2 hours.

I put Esther in a baby back pack that Russell hand made, and went to town.

I stopped at a hair dresser.

They admired my long strong blonde hair, the owner said; "We do wigs, we will buy your hair for 40 Suisse Francs".

In the 60s that was good money. I let them cut my hair very short, and took the money and went to buy a lot of baby food, and other stuff. Esther was more important to me than my hair.

The beginning of August the snow started to fall. People in the mountains hurry up to go back to town.

Russell came back with difficulty since it was slippery with the snow. He was worried sick about baby and me. But everything was just fine. When he saw my hair, he was in shock.

Asking; "What happened to your hair?"

I told him; "I sold it for baby food and it is better for Esther not to have my hair in her face especially when I feed her, and I needed the money."

He said; "You look different but good, it will grow back. It is like having another wife!"

Chapter 6

ROME

The money was diminishing and the best cost of living was in Italy so we decided to go live in Rome.

Russell rented a penthouse near the Appia Antica. Esther was 8 months old. Russell's Mother came to visit us, from Montreal, she was over 70 years old. Russell never had a close relationship with his mother as he was brought up with governesses and maids. He was 12 years old when his father died. His mother was always on the go, playing golf and going to formal parties and events. She never cooked a meal.

After her husband died, she sold all her properties in Boston and moved to Montreal.

Russell instructed me not to be familiar with his mother, to approach her with reverence.

When he came back from the airport with her, I welcomed them from the stairs then ran down to her to give her a big hug and told her, how wonderful it was of her to make such a long trip to come to visit us, all the while ignoring the very concerned look on Russell's face.

His mother smiled, she was enthusiastic about baby Esther, and wanted her to be baptized. I soon went to the Catholic church to have a meeting with the head priest.

The priest said because Russell was divorced and a Protestant and the fact that we did not get married in a church, we are excommunicated from the church and he cannot baptize Esther, but being Catholic and not divorced, he would accept 50,000 lire for redemption to go ahead and baptize Esther.

WHAT?!!!

No such thing is written in the Bible. I told Elisabeth Russell's mother, who was Protestant, but because I was Catholic, she insisted not to worry and that Esther needed to be baptized like her mother was, and paid the priest.

She bought a beautiful long white baby dress for this occasion.

The day of the baptism, our friends came and were appointed to be the God parents. Esther was already 8 months old and clearly demonstrated she was not happy with the priest. As he held her up in his hands to present her to God and praying a blessing over her, she grabbed his neck garment and shook it with all her strength. The priest started to pray the blessing over her very fast, and gave Esther to the Godparents to hold.

I was brought up Catholic and went to a private Catholic school. Though after I lived with Russell, I no longer went to the Catholic church.

In 1965, my sister was in a coma and my family had an evangelist pray over her and miraculously, she was instantly healed. This changed my family's hearts and opened my eyes about the meaning of the power of the blood of Jesus Christ that was shed for us on the cross. It was my sister who gave me my first Bible. I would read it, and from time to time, became more in love with the Lord but then I would revert and become lukewarm.

Russell studied the scriptures in the Bible before I met him. He stated that since it is a historic book, educated people, such as the American presidents, read the Bible, as It is the most published book in the entire world.

My mother in-law and I got along very well.

One day she said to Russell; "Tonight you are in charge of Esther. Mimi and I, we are going to the Opera, "Madame Butterfly" is playing and we are going."

When we came home from the play, I re-enacted the play for Russell in a comic yet tragic parody that made Russell explode in laughter.

I really liked his mother and she liked me.

She went back home and that was the last time Russell and I saw her.

It was winter time and Esther was almost 2 years old. I decided to go find some portrait commissions for Russell to work. I put on my elegant black Astrakhan fur coat, and carried an oil painting portrait of me wearing a white tutu that Russell painted, as an example of his work.

I went to a night club to solicit the leading show performers and was able to come back with two big photographs of the subjects wanting their portraits painted by Russell. It worked out great, since they did not have the time to come to pose, and Russell did not want to have these ladies from the night clubs in our home, but he needed the money. The two girls were very satisfied with their portraits.

The next month, the money was gone. I had to go look for work again, since Russell kept drinking and smoking cigarettes and used every last bit we had.

The director of the Piccadilly was very nice to me. He asked why I don't go back into show business instead of walking the streets of Rome at night. He said I would make a better income if I would go back to show business. He offered me an immediate contract of one month. I told him I would talk first to my husband before signing.

Russell objected, so I told him; "It's either that or you must accept the job offer in the private airport as an instructor pilot, because your painting career is not bringing enough income and we don't have money to finance the art gallery for your exhibitions."

Russell said; "I cannot be an instructor pilot anymore, I cannot stop drinking, I can't put people's life in danger, I know I am unstable."

I got to work, making two beautiful costumes and new innovative choreographies. The director was nice to me and favored my performances.

After a month, an agent offered me to pose for illustrated romance books.

I was then introduced to Sergio Ricci, the director producer of the Italian Television, and he said I needed to dye my hair black. In those days we only had black and white T V's. So, I dyed my hair black and went to the beach every day to get tanned to dance with a famous Afro-Cuban ballet.

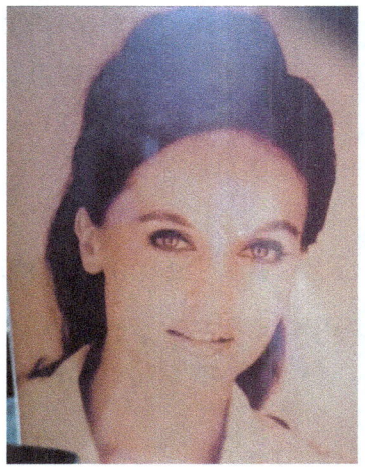

Sergio was very nice to me he took me to a restaurant we have diner before bringing me back home. It was late. We kissed good night, like we kiss everybody in show business.

Russell was watching from the terrace he came down the stairs and grabbed me by my hair pulling me up the stairs; he started beating me up and calling me names.

I protested trying to explain that nothing was going on with Sergio, he called me a liar. Russell was drunk and when he was drinking, he was crazy.

Our home was made with a lot of marble stone. I fell under the beating of Russell right on the marble border of the window. I got up to try to run and hide, but did not scream, I did not want to wake up Esther. It was a nightmare.

Russell never was so out of control. I was scared... out of fuel finally he went to sleep. I was unconscious in a puddle of blood.

The next day Russell was worried, he thought he killed me. My face was disfigured, swollen with a broken nose and swollen black eyes. He was putting cold compresses on my face. Esther was questioning what happened.

I told her; "Maman fell down the stairs, you must never go on the stairs alone."

I had an appointment for a meeting in the late afternoon, for a TV shot. For hours I tried everything I knew to diminish the swelling. It was better but impossible to make it disappear. I put a good amount of make-up, a large black hat and big sunglasses, and went to the meeting.

Sergio inspected me. I told him I fell on the marble stairs.

Sergio said; "If your family is important to you, you must choose, you don't get black eyes falling on the marble, broken nose maybe."

I chose my family. We stayed good friends.

I was doing only photos for romance magazines.

I was able to take Esther with me, from 8 am until 4 pm every day. Esther will hold onto my legs during shootings. The photographer was working from the top to my head to my hip, so Esther will not be in the shots. Italians are very family oriented they love children.

The next role I played, was a nun in a penitentiary. That was good for Esther because I wore a long heavy dress and Esther was able to hide inside.

That was 1968, I was pregnant again and Russell was sure that it was not from him because I was always on the go and we did not have much sex. I swore to him he was the only man in my life and I respected my marriage commitment.

I reminded him, the reason he did not trust me was because, he was the one who was not faithful and I was the one, who found him in Milano in bed with Sylvia, one of my friends.

During the 8 months of my pregnancy, Russell treated me like dirt. I kept working for 6 months, terribly stressed out, very little sleep, taking care of Esther and paying all the bills.

Russell's drinking was worse every month but he kept painting and got to do an exhibition of his work at an art gallery called "La Sulla".

Chapter 7

THE SPIRIT NEVER DIES

Doctor Alicino was the top gynecologist in Italy. All the celebrities like Sophia Loren, went to him. He had a well-known private clinic in Rome. He wanted to do my second C. Section as soon as possible. I was about 8 months pregnant. Russell was always drunk. He drove me to the front door of the clinic and pushed me out of the car.

He said; "I wish you dead with your bastard child who will surely have black hair and dark eyes!"

He was so sure that it was not his baby I was carrying, but that the father was the TV director, Sergio Ricci.

The nurse was surprised to see me alone in comparison to the others who came in with a bunch of relatives. She asked me where my family was and I told her my family was in France.

She took me in a room to prepare me for surgery happening the next morning.

I was alone, stressed out, thinking about Esther. (My mother and our friend, Sina from Switzerland, came 2 days later to take care of Esther.)

I had not had a real good night's sleep for months, because of the bad treatment from my alcoholic husband.

The next morning, I was strapped in on the operation table. The anesthetist injected me with more than according to my weight, because of my stress levels.

I was repeating; "Please don't let me die! I have a 22 months baby girl who needs me."

The anesthetist said; "Don't worry relax you will not finish counting to 3 that you will be sleeping."

But instead, I was talking to the staff.

Doctor Alicino was waiting to open me up, he told me previously, that he will make a nice invisible incision right on the top of my first C section, which was done in Switzerland by the best surgeon. He said it will be a nice bikini cut.

He asked the anesthetist; "Why is she not sleeping?"

The anesthetist answered; "I don't understand!".

There were two surgeons and four medical assistants around me, one held my hand, another one held my head. They had to go fast to save the baby because the baby was the one absorbing all the anesthesia.

The surgeon opened me up like a pig. A large cut opening my stomach, to be able to take the baby out fast and save the baby life. It was not a nice bikini cut.

I felt my mouth was stretching up right to my ears in a silent scream. The pain was so incredible that it paralyzed my voice.

I used to say mental pain was worse than physical pain. I don't say that anymore. This was horrible. I felt my heart exploding in a thousand pieces. I saw myself ejected out of my body. Then...There was no more physical pain, I did not have a body anymore. I was speeding in a tunnel and I could see a bright light at the end of the tunnel, but I knew in my spirit, I will never get there. All my life was like a movie before my eyes.

Everything I wanted when I was young. To be a ballerina, get admiration, fame, luxurious car, furs, jewelry. I got all that and for what? I was dead. A terrible sensation struck me.

ALL MY LIFE WAS A WASTE!

I was so sorry, I recognized the world was my God, I did not obey the first commandment;

"LOVE THE LORD YOUR GOD WITH ALL YOUR HEART WITH ALL YOUR SOUL WITH ALL YOUR STRENGTH AND YOU SHALL NOT HAVE ANY OTHER GOD BEFORE ME."

The words of my devoted mother came strongly in my spirit;

"Mimi, if one day you are in danger, call the blood of Jesus Christ to cover you and cry out to God. God will see only the blood of his son, Jesus, not you."

I remembered what happened to me in 1965 when I went to visit my family, after the miraculous healing of my sister. We had prayer meetings in my parent's home. The Holy Spirit was present.

Like Jesus said "IF TWO OR THREE PRAY IN MY NAME I WILL BE THERE."

One evening I was so touched, in the middle of the praise and worship, Gill, a young evangelist started to pray very loudly in a strange language. We knew he only spoke French. I was shocked as I could not believe he would make such a fool out of himself.

My mother was lost in a deep worship. Right then, I started to tremble so hard that I fell on the chair behind me.

I became blind, a light cloud covered me and a white baby face appeared with no tongue and no eyes. Then, I was able to see again but my body did not stop trembling.

For three days, I walked in another dimension feeling very holy. A few days later, another evangelist, Michel, came to visit and I told him the vision.

He said to me; "Did you ask God what that means?"

I was puzzled! "What? Me? ask God???"

Michel said; "Let us pray and ask God to reveal to you what He wanted to tell you."

Michel's eyes closed, got the interpretation of the vision, his face and his voice changed.

He spoke loudly; "This baby face is you in the Spirit. You don't have a tongue to speak and no eyes to see about the things of God yet."

Wow! Immediately, I remembered Gill. I thought he was a fool speaking in tongues. I repented and never again disbelieved speaking in the Holy Spirit.

I WAS BORN AGAIN! But why I was not in heaven? Evangelists proclaim: If you accept Jesus to be your redeemer, you will go to heaven no matter what. The blood of Jesus who was shed on the cross and died for ALL my sins! Past, Present and Future......

Why was I in this tunnel? and I felt in my spirit that I was lost forever.

Jesus said; "IF YOU LOVE ME! YOU WILL OBEY ME." I did not obey Jesus, I lived in sin, I put my children before God, I put show business before God, I put my will before His will. So now I was lost forever.

It was too late to repent.

But I begged God anyway:

"God please in the name of the blood of your son Jesus, please give me another chance for my baby Esther, please Lord, for Esther......
for Esther."

I was back in a very painful body, just before they were going to put me in the fridge. The blood was running out of my belly, they did not close me correctly since they believed me to be dead.

The nurse called the doctor yelling; "She is alive!"

Then again without anesthesia, the doctor put more metal staples to close my stomach to stop the bleeding. Russell came during the night. He was drunk. Baby Eric was under an oxygen tent.

Russell said; "It was easy to spot my first son in the nursery. He is the only gold head in the sea of black hair babies, all the nurses are around his bed, they call him "Little Prince." I think he looks like me......I am so sorry for what I did to you."

The doctor told him that I will probably not make it through the night.

Since that day I died, my love for him died also. We continued to live under the same roof for the children's sake. He had his section of the house, I had mine.

Yes! That day, January 14, 1969, was the most incredible memorable day of my life. To have died and come back in this life. To see my first son!

It was so hard to come back to a normal life after that. I was dead and I came back in this world to be a mother for my children.

NOW I KNOW WITHOUT A DOUBT THAT THE SPIRIT NEVER DIES.

I was not able to sleep, I had nightmares almost every night for months, seeing me traveling in that tunnel forever in regret.

Slowly after months, I started to get my strength back...But did not stop to think every day and night of my death experience.

I started to have a strong hatred against men.

The more you hold on to anger, bitterness, rage, the more you open yourself to physical disease.

My question was, why did I not go to heaven if I was born again?

I read Mathew 7:22 "MANY WILL SAY TO ME IN THAT DAY, "LORD, LORD, HAVE WE NOT PROPHESIED IN YOUR NAME, CAST OUT DEMONS IN YOUR NAME AND DONE MANY WONDERS IN YOUR NAME?" (23) AND THEN I WILL DECLARE TO THEM: "I NEVER KNEW YOU, DEPART FROM ME YOU WHO PRACTICE LAWLESSNESS."

I just lived for myself.

Chapter 8

ESTHER BABY STAR

After almost a year, I went back to my agent to get a job to do more photos romance story magazine, so I could be able to take my children with me. Esther was 3 years old. When my agent saw Esther, she told me to take her immediately to have an audition for a movie with Catherine Deneuve and Marcello Mastroianni, to play their daughter.

When we arrived, the place was packed with hundreds of moms and their adorable little girls, waiting to be chosen. They had just passed a law that film producers needed to use Italian Citizens instead of foreigners. When I saw the crowd of beautiful little girls, I turned around to walk back out the door, but a gentleman stopped us asking why we were leaving.

I told him; "I don't know why my agent sent me here, we are not Italian, I am not going to waste hours for nothing."

He said; "It is not a beauty contest, we are looking for young children who can act natural in front of the camera, and artist moms to work with."

He took us through another door right to the cameraman and the producer room.

Esther followed all the instructions, then the cameraman came out from the back of his camera. He was a nice gentleman, but he had a beard and Esther never saw a man with a beard before, she got scared and put her head against my chest and refused to look at him.

I said; "I am sorry that will not work, Esther is scared of your beard."

The producer liked Esther he had already seen lots of children for two days. He said Esther was the best choice, he told the cameraman to go shave his beard.

Esther became a little star. Esther also did advertisement on TV for spaghetti sauce.

Eric, nine months, also got a part of playing the baby portion of the role Esther got in the movie. Esther got used to being the center of everyone's attention, and receiving gifts. I was playing the maid in the movie to be near Esther. The money was very good, but to be working from 8 am to 8 pm, was hard on little Esther. I was adamant about putting her down for a nap every day at 3 o'clock, but one day the producer insisted for Esther not to have her nap and to continue filming. Esther was so tired she started to cry. I walked up in the middle of the filming, grabbed Esther in my arms and left.

The producer came with the crew to our house. I told them the health of my daughter was more important than all the fame and the money in the world. The producer promised to respect her nap time and did some shooting in our home.

A few months after that......A period with no contract. I needed to go back to work in the night clubs to provide for the family.

Most of the night clubs were controlled by the Mafia. They were so elegant and well-mannered that it was difficult to differentiate them from the rest of the crowd. Except when one night I found out who was who. Everything seemed fine, and the next thing you know, people shooting at each other. Glasses and bottles flying, all the musicians in the orchestra jumping behind the curtain and every girl hiding under a table. After the noise stopped, I came out of the dressing room. The sight was shocking, all the waiters were cleaning the mess very fast and the Orchestra started playing again like nothing had happened.

During that time, I met a French young woman, Christine, she became a close friend. She was an outstanding opera singer from Paris, she came to Rome to practice with a renowned voice coach.

The Opera in Rome did not have any opening at the moment, and the only option to get work, was to work in a night club. We ended up working in the same place. She would come to our home and I would go to her place, sometimes to listen to her practice her voice with a maestro from the Opera.

She was amazing, she could sing soprano so high with perfect pitch and then go deep down low alto, like Maria Callas. Sincerely I believe she was better.

One day Christine came asking if she could stay in our home. She was trembling with fear. She explained to me that, the good-looking gentlemen, who asked her out for dinner the week before, came to her home with another nice-looking young man, Vincent, to take her out for the day. They went to the beach and then they invited her inside a lavish beach home. They opened the bar and started drinking, then they used cocaine and wanted her to take some, but she refused. They did not like that she would not join them, and became mad. She wanted to leave but they refused to drive her back home. All of a sudden, they heard the arrival of a few cars parking in front of the home and could hear voices of people approaching. The two guys grabbed her by the hand and jumped out of the balcony and ran on the beach.

Only then she realized that was not their house and the owner had just arrived with a bunch of guests. Christine told me she walked a long distance before she was able to find a taxi, and came to my home, but she was too scared to go back to her place. She stayed to live in our place.

Her mother came to visit from Paris for a week. Christine was divorced. Her ex-husband was one of the conductors of the Opera Orchestra in Paris. She told me what a disappointment it was for her when she found her husband in bed with a man. She was heartbroken.

We could talk to each other for hours about things we kept private and this was a good outlet for the both of us.

We needed to go back to work in the night club but we knew Vincent and Roberto would be there. Vincent insisted to invite me to his table. I refused.

The director pleaded with me; "Please if you will not accept his invitation, he is going to start a fight."

So, I went. Vincent was proud to be in the Mafia. He was crazy about me and would shower me with jewelry. I told him I was married with two children and it would be best to not pursue me.

His reply was; "I want you, and I always get everything I want. Your husband obviously does not love you to make you work in a night club. I will make you my queen and keep you in a castle, cover you with diamond and gold, and I will kill anyone that tries to stop me, including your husband and kids. You will be mine!"

I was scared, but I laughed pretending he was telling a joke, but those guys were criminals and on drugs, and I needed to get rid of them, but how?........They controlled most of the night clubs, and they gave so much money to the police to not interfere. Money is the source of all evil. Money corrupts.

Christine went back to Paris with her mother. I had no one to talk to, or look to for protection. I finished the last show and sneaked out of the back door to go to my car in a deserted small street.

Very fast I got inside my car. Right then Vincent shows up and sits in the passenger seat. I quickly opened my door to try to get out of the car, but I was pushed inside by Roberto who came to sit in the driver's side next to me and started the car, speeding away from the club. I was stuck in the middle, I started to cry and begged Vincent to let me go, they both laughed, so I stopped crying, and tried to think how to escape.

We arrived to their home they left the key in my car. They dragged me up the stairs. Inside the house was all kinds of drugs on the table with syringes.

Roberto went to take more drugs. Vincent pushed me on the bed, I told him in a calm voice. Let me take a shower first, he agreed. I ran to the door but before I was out of the door, Vincent grabbed me and threw me on the bed. I fought, with all my strength.

The book shelf fell on the bed. Roberto came to the room but fell to the floor he passed out cold. Foam was coming out of his mouth from overdosing.

Vincent did not care about him. He was fighting with me and raped me. He soon also finally lost consciousness and passed completely out.

All beat up, trembling and crying, I ran to my car, driving like mad. It was 4 in the morning and I saw a police car, I stopped my car and told the policeman what happened and to go to arrest my aggressors.

He said; "I don't get involved with the Mafia, every time we arrest one of them for a serious crime, they get released the next day. Money talks and they have people working for them everywhere. You should be happy to be alive, every day we find young girls dead on the beach. Why were you out in the middle of the night alone anyway?"

I did not want to listen to one more word. I pushed the accelerator and went home.

I took a long bath. Did not say a word to Russell or anyone, I kept my ordeal to myself. The police man was right, why was I out alone at night? Why? Why! Why!?

To make enough money to pay for the bills and feed my children, because my husband was not providing anything anymore for us.

I called in sick for the next two days.

A deep hatred started to grow bigger and bigger in my heart for men. I wanted vengeance!

I went back to work. After the last show, a gang of drug dealers invited me and against my will, I had to accept their invitation to please the director who was always good to me.

I danced with the leader who was Vincent's rival. I did not say a word to him. Just smiled. As I looked over at the table where the rest of the gang sat, I saw one putting something in my champagne glass.

After the dance, he leads me to their table and hands me the glass to toast. I pretend to be drunk and fall down over the table, breaking all the glasses and spilling over the bottle of champagne. They insulted me in Italian. I was laughing, pretending not to speak Italian and said that I needed to change my dress who was soaking wet.

I stayed in the dressing room, waiting for Vincent who came every night about midnight. Then, I saw him arriving. I went to him and told him what the rival gang did to me, and told him they tried to drug me to kidnap me.

Vincent was furious and went to talk to his guys. Then went to the leader of the gang and told him he was going to kill him. The two gangs started to fight. The director begged them to go outside. They all went out. I was hoping they would kill each other so I will be free from Vincent.

My belief was from the Old Testament: "AN EYE FOR AN EYE."

Yes! It worked!!! Since that night Vincent disappeared.

I started to feel free again. Christine my friend came back from Paris and together we enjoyed the beauty of living in Rome.

I started to get worried when I didn't have my period. I went through a difficult time and maybe it caused this irregularity...... but more time passed and now I was sure I was pregnant. I had not slept with my husband since Eric was born, it had been almost two years.

No! to be pregnant from a drug addict and a criminal! It was absolutely out of the question. I asked a friend who was gynecologist to check me, and he confirmed my worst expectation.

I asked him to give me an abortion because not only did I not want the baby from being raped, but my last C. Section, I died on the operation table. I had my two beautiful children and they needed me.

The doctor was a Catholic and abortion was against the law in Italy. He refused to abort me. There were a bunch of speculums, instruments for female examination, near me in the doctor's office, when the doctor turned his back to wash his hands, I stole one, and put it in my purse. Got dressed very fast and slammed the door. I was so mad at him because he refused to help me.

My life was in danger. I was mad at God. Why should I pay with my death for what was done to me against my will?

Or was this my punishment for wishing and orchestrating Vincent's death? I could never forgive Vincent for what he did to me. I wanted vengeance, I wanted to make every man pay for my pain.

I stopped praying. I stopped reading the Bible.

God is the King of Kings, the Almighty everlasting God. I should worship him and respect him and adore him, and what ever happened to me was orchestrated by the evil one, to do everything to turn me away from God.

That is why it is so important to read the Bible. The Bible not only speaks about the blessings but about people who mess up a lot and the forgiveness and mercy of God when we repent.

I did not repent, instead I asked Christine to help me to do the abortion using the speculum. She poked the baby bag and I started bleeding but not much. I felt weak soon after but refused to faint. After resting, I went back to my home feeling sick for days. I was continuing to bleed but the fetus had not come out. I started to feel weaker and soon a fever emerged.

I asked Russell to take me with the children to my sister's house in Switzerland. She was a kinesiologist neuroscience therapist, and her husband owned a luxurious hotel on the lake of Lugano, a very selected touristic place.

Russell saw that I was very sick, but I never told him why. We left immediately. My sister was glad to see us and to finally introduce us to her husband as she ordered a feast in their restaurant.

As the feast kept coming and all sorts of beautifully arranged food adorned the table,

Lydia, my sister, asked me what was wrong with me and saw that I was not eating. I asked her if I could go to the hotel room she had reserved for us. I had terrible cramps and started to bleed. Lydia concerned came to my room and found me bleeding in the floor bathroom. She immediately called her doctor. The doctor arrived within minutes. I explained what had taken place. He said I needed to go immediately to the hospital to have a medically assisted miscarriage as the fever was high and I needed intravenous antibiotics for the infection I begged the doctor and my sister to not tell Russell about it, because I was not pregnant from him, and told them about the rape.

The hospital in Lugano, put me on intravenous antibiotics. I was in so much pain, during the night I had the miscarriage alone in the room. A nurse came to check on me and discovered me in a bath of blood in agony. The fetus was out. The nurse said it was a boy. Quickly she took me to the operating room.

The surgeon cleaned me and said I was not out of danger, because of the infection caused by me trying to abort myself.

After five days, the doctor said I needed to go back to the hospital in the next town I was going, until I will be out of danger.

The doctor said; "I just talked to your husband and explained to him to take you as soon as possible in the care of a good doctor."

I started to tremble and said; "He is going to kill me. My husband did not know I was raped."

He said; "No, he was calm and assured me that he will take good care of you."

Russell without a word opened the car door. He started driving then he exploded. He called me a lot of horrible names, then he beat me badly. I was so sick I did not say a word. We arrived to my sister's home where Esther and Eric had stayed.

Lydia saw me. She looked at Russell in a despicable way and told him sternly to be ashamed of himself. That it was his fault all of this happened. Had he taken care of his family and provided, I would have been home with the children and would not have gotten raped.

Chapter 9

MESSED UP FOR LIFE

We packed to go to my parent's home town in France. My cousin was a surgeon cardiologist and his wife was a gynecologist. They took care of me with an intensive treatment and never commented about my private life. After a long recovery, we went back to our home in Rome. I was not able to work.

I did not expect God to forgive me. I recognized I had broken almost all of THE TEN COMMANDMENTS.

1, I put my children before God.

2, I lied.

3, I did not keep the Sabbath holy.

4, I had an abortion. Meaning I was a murderer.

5, I committed adultery.

6, I stole.

7, I coveted.

It is written; "THE WAGES OF SIN IS DEATH."

I accepted that I deserved to be sent to hell, so I did not have a problem to hate and manipulate men, now I was lost. I saw myself so dirty. I would not dare to utter the precious name of the Lord. I wanted vengeance before I died and make every man responsible for my punishment.

I continued to hemorrhage and was in pain since the abortion.

I gave myself 2 shots of anti-hemorrhage solution and one shot of B12 for energy every day before show time, as I, of course had to work again. I never told anyone about my condition, only the doctors. I covered myself with heavy makeup, a smile and beautiful attire.

I was a pretender. It was show-time every minute of my life. Only after the children went to bed, in secret, I would deflate like a balloon. And break down.

I got contracts in different parts of Italy. I visited a specialist that said I needed surgery because there was a cancerous growth in my uterus. A consequence of the abortion. My red blood cells were very low. I needed to build up my strength before I could have surgery.

I continued to perform in the theatre and night club to be able to pay the bills, plus pay for the art gallery and organizing exhibitions for Russell and other artists. The expenses were huge, and not enough profit.

I did not know enough about the word of God, to comprehend the immense sacrifice of Jesus on the cross. I thought my sins was unpardonable, I judged myself the way I was taught in Catholic school. More about penitence.

Not about that Christ died to redeem the ungodly "FOR BY GRACE YOU HAVE BEEN SAVED TROUGH FAITH AND THAT NOT OF YOURSELVES IT IS THE GIFT OF GOD." (Ephesians; 2: 8)

"GRACE" What is Grace? "Undeserved favor, grace cannot be earned, it is freely given."

One memorable day, I got a visit from Duke Emmanuel, accompanied by two beautiful young American missionaries. Emanuel was always looking for something interesting. He spoke English, French and Italian. He was eager to introduce them to me, Rachel the tall one looked like a model and the other one, Faithy had a radiant face with the most incredible smile. She carried her guitar. She asked me if she could sing a song for me. Faithy, playing her guitar, started to sing. Something was so different about her voice, her eyes closed, every word was speaking directly to my heart. Her face was shining with the Holy Spirit. I started to be deeply moved like never before. Something melted inside of me. My mask of the perfect pretender vanished...and I was not able to stop the tears flowing from messing up my makeup. I just cried uncontrollably.

The words of her song were; "HOW LONG HAVE YOU BEEN WAITING FOR SOMEONE WHO REALLY LOVES YOU...FOR SOMEONE WHO REALLY CARES...FOR SOMEONE WHO WILL NEVER LEAVE YOU! HIS NAME IS JESUS... JESUS... JESUS! She repeated the same words over and over. She finished the song brilliantly with. NEVER! NEVER! NEVER LEAVE YOU!"

Under the spotlights, I was a beautiful doll. All my admirers lusted after me. They did not care about my soul. Yes! I had my name and pictures in magazines, at the cost of a tortured body, always in competition with others, making a good living for my children, Esther now five and Eric three years old. My husband was an alcoholic.

What started with Russell first looked like a beautiful dream or a fairy tale, then after a few years, it had turned into a nightmare.

I asked Faithy; "Why do you look so happy? You have no place to stay, no money, apparently you have nothing in this world, but you look like you have won millions, what is it? I want what you have!"

Faithy's answer was; "I have Jesus in my heart! When Jesus the Christ lives in your heart you have joy and peace in every situation. You can have that too.

Jesus said; "IN THE WORLD YOU WILL HAVE TRIBULATION; BUT BE OF GOOD CHEER, I HAVE OVERCOME THE WORLD!"

Faithy was on a mission to obey what Jesus said, in Mark 16:15 "GO INTO ALL THE WORLD AND PREACH THE GOSPEL TO EVERY CREATURE."

The Revolution for Jesus movement, were made up of groups going into different parts of the world and trying to bring lost young hippies to salvation through sharing the gospel. She sang and preached in public places, sat on the floor with the destitute and hippies, hugged them, prayed with them and fed them. I watched her, deeply touched to see someone living with so much love for the lost. I admired her courage.

I told her; "I can never do what you do, it's insane!"

Her answer was; "You will do that and more when the love of Jesus becomes real to you."

I never thought about Jesus that way, I was too self-centered, only focused on me and my children.

To really love Jesus? to obey and worship Him as my Savior? to see Him tortured and dying on the cross for me? to be forgiven from all my sins and have an eternal life in paradise with God?

When all that will become REAL to me, I will be able to say; "LORD, I LOVE YOU!"

Faithy lived in abnegation of everything.

She said; "My husband is an evangelist in England and I haven't seen him in a year because there are too many lost souls and the need is great for more evangelists. It is a spiritual war against Satan and his evil angels, a 24 hours battle. Just like an army we cannot be slowed down by our own emotions and problems. To be sorry for myself, that is a demonic emotion...

We cannot be pitiful and powerful, the power of Jesus Christ in us makes us over-comers. We are a Royal Priesthood, eternal life with

God is our destination and we want to bring a lot of souls to heaven with us, that is a competition with our adversary, the evil one.'

These words inspired me to help in some way.

I transformed my Art Gallery to a free coffee house.

Russell came back from a trip and freaked out. The gallery was overcrowded with missionaries ministering to a bunch of hippies.

Russell came back down the stairs from the apartment.

Yelling; "There are two girls in my bed with big balloons in their stomachs! What's going on here?" (Referencing two pregnant girls.)

Russell grabbed the guitar from one evangelist and threw everybody out.

I tried to stop him, but everyone apologized and left.

I told Russell; "You forget, this is my art gallery and I will do what I want. For the first time in my life, I feel at peace. You only came back to rip me off again."

He said; "Are you mad! I will prefer to see you go with your Italian prince than to have my children mixed up with a bunch of fanatics, lunatic, dirty so-called Christians! They are going to strip you of every penny you have and then forget about you."

I told him; "That is not worse than what you are doing to me I prefer to feed the needy than to pay for your drinking party."

The next day Faithy and Rachel came with Duke Emanuel and asked me if I would translate for Faithy at a communist rally that night. I accepted.

Seven young evangelists from Faithy's staff came to report that they were escorted out after they started to sing about Jesus. A guard on a motorcycle stopped them and was very rude to them.

I told them to come with me, and faced the guard on the motorcycle. I asked his name, he reluctantly said;

"My name is Gianni"

I asked him; "Gianni! if you believe that communism has more power than Christianity, what are you so afraid of? Do you know who started communism?"

He answered; "Karl Marx in 1850."

I replied; "Do you know that Karl Marx was a Jew? To be exact communism started 2000 years ago with a Jew whose name is JESUS THE CHRIST, HE GAVE HIS LIFE FOR YOU TO BE FREE FROM SIN."

Gianni was mad; "Don't give me that crap and don't say that name here!"

I told him I was going to report him.
He said; "Go head!"

Just then I heard my name called. I was pleased to see Sergio Ricci, the director of all the TV stations.
Sergio was surprised to see me without makeup, wearing a long dress, vanilla cream that was a Faithy gift to me for translating next to her on the podium. She always wore long dresses.

He asked; "What role are you going to play? Hmm...There is something different about you."
I told him about re-dedicating myself to Christ and quickly explained the issue with the guard.
Sergio told us to go to the podium #4.

Faithy, along with a couple of professional evangelist musicians, began playing songs. Then, Faithy preached as I translated in Italian. They finished off with a few more songs.

Gianni stayed and watched the whole time. During the singing, Sarah and I witnessed to Gianni.

We sang to him a verse in the bible, John 3:16 and we inserted his name; "FOR GOD SO LOVED "GIANNI" THAT HE GAVE HIS ONLY SON, JUST FOR YOU, BECAUSE HE LOVES YOU!". Gianni was so moved that he accepted Jesus on the spot.

I started to feel very sick and could hardly stand on my feet. Faithy was very concerned and asked why I was so pale. I told her I needed to do my shots.

At home, Faithy helped me into bed and told me she would pray for me to be healed.

I said; "No it's ok, I have sinned so much and deserve to suffer. I know I am going to heaven now, and that is good enough for me."

That was all the teaching I remembered from all those years being Catholic. We needed to suffer to please God. Today when I think of it, it sounds absurd to imagine a loving God that would enjoy his children suffering.

Faithy said; "Mimi, Jesus paid it all on the cross. Healing and salvation. To refuse healing is an offence to God. He paid such a great price because He loves you."

She was in tears to see my ignorance about the grace of God.
Grace means gift... an unmerited favor.

She said; "Please let me pray for you, the only thing you must do is to believe that God loves you."

It was hard for me to imagine God loving me. I did not love myself and I did not love God.

Faithy prayed a short prayer with compassion. I felt something like a warm wave going inside of me and going out.

The blood felt like it had suddenly stopped gushing out of me. I jumped on my feet, feeling electrified. I was lit up, like some indestructible powerful force possessed me. I ran down the stairs screaming;

"I feel great! I am healed! Jesus healed me!"

To be healed by the precious blood of Jesus Christ and to feel the presence of the Lord in me was the most amazing thing I had ever felt! all the money in the world could not buy this feeling.

That day, everything changed. I discovered that God was near and that He cared about me. Money could not fix my body and my broken heart, but the blood of Jesus did! I just saw God manifested in my life. I never felt a love like this, it was divine. I really fell in love with the Lord, I was ready to live and die for my Lord because He was worthy.

I asked Faithy; "Can I join the Revolution for Jesus?"

Faithy said; "You would be such a blessing for us but I must tell you, it is not about just like the song we sing "I want to be like Jesus" and then go home to rest. We live the book of Acts, we share everything. We give everything we possess, no more comfort. It will cost you everything to become a disciple of Jesus, a complete surrender to be an instrument in the hands of God. You must pray and recognize the cost before you make your commitment."

Chapter 10

MY ITALIAN PRINCE

PSALM 107: 20 "HE SENT HIS WORD AND HEALED THEM AND DELIVERED THEM FROM THEIR DESTRUCTIONS."

For days I meditated on those words. Yes! God delivered me from my destruction. I also meditated on my past.

I had accepted invitations from men. Prince Frederico would do anything to try to take me to his bed, from Napoli to Rome he pursued me. He will not accept if a girl resisted his advances.

Then there was Baron Luciano, he did bring me a ring, but I said No!

He said; "why you don't like me?"

I told him maybe if you lose 20 pounds I will like you. He disappeared for two weeks.

Luciano came back and said; "I lost 20 pounds in a private clinic in Milano for you! Now do you like me?"

He looked so weak I thought he was going to faint. He had big dark circles under his eyes. He was using his handkerchief to wipe his face from perspiration.

I stood up and said; "You looked better before!" and left. I enjoyed making men suffer.

But after Faithy prayer over me, most of this hatred against men changed. I realized they are Just like me, lost.

"I WAS LOST AND NOW I'M FOUND, WAS BLIND BUT NOW I SEE!"

It was time to meditate on the word of God because Jesus is the word of God coming in the flesh to instruct us about the character of his father God.

The next day, Frederic, the prince from Napoli, called to invite me with Esther and Eric to dinner. He said it was important he really liked my children's behavior.

He said to them; "You behave like a prince and a princess more seemingly than my own niece and I would be proud to be your father, Mimi what do you say?"

I laughed and said; "Of course my dear, but there is a little thing you forgot. I am married!"

Frederic's answer was; "I have my source of information and according to our Italian law, you were not married in the church, so for us you are not married. My lawyer will have no problem taking care of any interference and Russell will have money to do what he likes best. Painting, alcohol and women."

I asked; "Why do you want to marry me? I am a show girl not an aristocrat."

He said; "You are an artist, that is the gold key to every door. Do you remember the first time we met in Napoli? After the show, I invited you to my table with my entourage, you refused to sit with me, I told you who I was, and to sit down.

You said; "You are a prince in Napoli! And you tell your people to obey you, but I am the Queen of the show and I tell you GO TO HELL!"

Then you left. That was the first time in my life that a girl talked to me like that. I wanted to kill you.

I was so offended in front of my friends. But I was smitten. I made a bet that I would have you in my yacht the next week. I lost. I sent roses, champagne. Nothing happened. My last chance is to marry you."

I was listening, thinking, now that the Lord healed me, I have a new opportunity to become a princess? I was wondering if this was God's answer for my future. I told Frederic I needed to pray about it.

The next day in the art gallery, the Bible study was about (Matthew 19:16 – 21) "GOOD TEACHER, WHAT GOOD THING SHALL I DO THAT I MAY HAVE ETERNAL LIFE?

JESUS SAID TO HIM; "WHY DO YOU CALL ME GOOD? NO ONE IS GOOD BUT ONLY ONE, BUT THAT IS GOD. BUT IF YOU WANT TO ENTER INTO LIFE, KEEP THE COMMANDMENTS."

THE YOUNG MAN SAID TO HIM; "ALL THESE THINGS I HAVE KEPT FROM MY YOUTH, WHAT DO I STILL LACK?"

JESUS SAID TO HIM; "IF YOU WANT TO BE PERFECT, GO SELL WHAT YOU HAVE AND GIVE IT TO THE POOR, AND YOU WILL HAVE A TREASURE IN HEAVEN, AND COME AND FOLLOW ME."

The lecture continued...... This particular scripture was exploding in my mind, and my heart was beating faster, it felt like birth pain.

I prayed, Lord please what do You want me to do?

Those words came strongly into my mind;

"WHAT WILL IT BE? YOUR ITALIAN PRINCE FREDERIC OR THE PRINCE OF ETERNAL LIFE JESUS THE CHRIST?"

God wanted me to choose, God never imposes His will.

Deeply in my heart I examined my life from the beginning and as long as I could remember, I recognize that nothing could bring such peace and inner joy than the presence of the Holy Spirit of God.

Now I knew that God loved me. Jesus manifested Himself to me and it was no longer a story book. He was real, but not only that, His spirit was living in me and I would never be alone again. I don't have to perform or impress Him. He loves me. He knows everything about me and He still loves me.

Frederic called. I told him I chose Jesus.

Suddenly my flesh was in torment, it was not easy to abandon the world.

I prayed; "Lord, I said I love you, and again you give me another chance! What is wrong with me, am I a phony?"

I was telling Faithy, that I was ready to join the Revolution for Jesus.

She said; "Mimi, if you choose to come live with us, you will have to give up all that you possess and walk in the spirit... because the only thing we can bring to heaven is souls."

I told her; "Jesus gave everything for me. I understand the enormous cost of the cross, I had a death experience in 1969, the physical pain was horrible and my Jesus went through torture on the cross so much more, for me.

I have had no mercy or love for my husband since 1969, I know I need to forgive him."

Faithy said; "Remember addiction to alcohol was Satan's work in Russell to destroy you and your family. Every addiction is an evil spirit, to make you a slave, that can destroy war heroes and the most talented people.

Satan uses what looks like nothing, just a little substance to kill your mind.

But if we turn to Jesus for help, it is hope. Most of our converts where professional musicians and singers addicted to drugs and alcohol and all kinds of sins, but they are free today serving God.

The inability to forgive is like a poison that destroys the soul and keeps us prisoner.

When you forgive, you deliver yourself, you will be free from resentment, the devil will not be able to torture you about this anymore."

I prayed; "O Lord please help me to forgive Russell...and to love him."

Just before I gave everything away, my agent called to offer me the best paid contract of my life!

I had a meeting with Faithy and the other leaders along with Emanuel the Duke, and told them what had happened.

I said; "I know that this money would be a big help for the Revolution for Jesus. I should make this my last show and then join the Revolution."

Everyone was enthusiastic about the money.

Faithy had her eyes closed praying in silence. She would not talk until she got an answer from the Holy Spirit. After minutes of silence.

Faithy finally Spoke; "Mimi, God wants you now. He can drop money from the sky if we need it, but God needs you now!"

I felt so much joy to know that God wanted me for His service, not my money like everybody else.

Faithy was a light in the middle of those people. She never made a decision without asking God and waiting for His answer. Sometimes it would take the whole day. That is why she was the leader, and the reason behind getting her name because she would only walk by faith in God and not by sight.

To hear the voice of the Lord, you must empty your mind of everything, to make room for the Lord to hear His voice. If we are only thinking about ourselves and our problems, we cannot hear the voice of the Lord.

The training was to memorize Bible verses all day long. To be really born again, is to love what Jesus said.

Our mind needed to be unloaded completely from our previous life and reloaded with the word of God. Jesus is the Word of God.

John 1: 1-5; "IN THE BEGINNING WAS THE WORD

AND THE WORD WAS WITH GOD,

AND THE WORD WAS GOD.

THE SAME WAS IN THE BEGINNING WITH GOD.

ALL THINGS WERE MADE BY HIM,

AND WITH HIM WAS NOT ANYTHING MADE THAT WAS MADE.

IN HIM WAS LIFE AND THE LIFE WAS THE LIGHT OF MEN.

AND THE LIGHT SHINES IN DARKNESS

AND THE DARKNESS COMPREHENDED IT NOT."

The people who know that, will never put a Bible on the floor or put stuff on the top of the Word of God.

The bible is not just a book. It's God speaking to us. The word of God is life for our soul.

In Jewish Temples, I was touched to see the way they respect the Holy Book. They kiss the book after they finish reading it and never put it upside-down, or put anything on the top of it, because they consider the Word of God precious.

Chapter 11

U TURN

Russell got an inheritance from his deceased mother. He and all his friends tried everything to dissuade me to join the Revolution for Jesus.

Knowing my passion for sport cars, he said he would buy me a Maserati if I dropped this crazy sect.

Maserati 1972

In 1970, I owned a 2600 Alfa Romeo, one of the fastest sport cars in Europe. I race at 4 am with guys in the deserted streets of Rome. Of course I won. But now I was ready to give it all away. Jesus became more important to me than any sport car.

One Rabbi used to say; "Never let your ambition take the place of God."

(Alfa Romeo2600)

2600 ALFA ROMEO 1970

I told Russell I was ready to move to a retreat as I already gave all my possessions away and for him to take what belongs to him.

Russell freaked out; "You cannot take my children with you! Esther is a child star and you and her have a contract with your agent."

I answered; "Esther is five years old. You are never there for her or Eric, Jesus healed me, so I can be alive and a mother to my children. Money did not heal me. Jesus loves me and he cares for me. You don't." (It was September 1972)

Russell talked to Esther; "Esther, you love to be a movie star, right? The people your mom is going with are very poor and that means if you go with her, you will have no more nice dresses, nice home, no more toys...You will be cold and hungry. But if you stay with your dad, you will have everything you like. What do you say?"

Esther without hesitation answered; "I want to be like mom not like you. But you can come with us, get ready."

Reluctantly he said; "I am going to drive my children to Certaldo. I want to see where you're taking my children."

The property was about 3 hours driving from Rome in Toscani. A mansion on 240 acres, with two farms and a hunting lodge, plus the manager's house, who was in charge of the property. This belonged to Duke Emanuel de Carnavero.

I took with me two pregnant young ladies and their three little children.

The big mansion was in a good condition, but the other houses needed a lot of repairs.

I stayed with the children and the young women in the mansion with Duke Emanuel, Faithy and Rachel.

Russell was satisfied to see where his children were and he went to stay in a hotel.

A week later, a big bus packed with young people arrived from London.

Faithy, surprised, started to cry of joy when she saw Joshua her husband. He was tall and strong and carried Faithy in his arms because she almost fainted from the surprise.

Thank God for all those guys coming to help fix all the other homes.

The big mansion did not look so big anymore.

Emanuel went back to Rome.

A month later, another bus came with more guys and a leader named Omar, who was fluent in English, French and Hungarian. He was able to repair anything and was a pro at printing literature, as that was necessary for distribution when we witnessed out. He was a good teacher, a musician and a very good singer.

The need for beds and blankets were great because it was chilly at the end of October. All those guys were sleeping on the floor in sleeping bags.

Faithy went on the road again pioneering new territory.

Her husband Joshua, assisted by Miguel and Omar, was in charge of about 80 adults plus 15 children, ages one to five.

The new Italian converts were spiritual babes. I was the only one that spoke fluent Italian.

Joshua thought I was spiritually mature enough to be the "Mother of the colony" for the new converts, and the Public Relations for the Revolution for Jesus.

The next day he called me and gave me a big list of all the needs, which included 50 beds, blankets, tables, chairs, sewing machines with fabric, baby supplies and on and on went the list.

I asked Joshua; "Do you have any money? I don't have any more money."

Joshua was in his forties, six feet tall, very athletic, with a big black beard. He started laughing very loudly.

He said; "Well Mimi, it is good that you cannot depend on your money anymore because now you can learn what it means to walk by faith. Come let's pray."

TO WALK BY FAITH TO GO SHOPPING???

I drove to Rome with Esther and Eric. We arrived in Rome late. I decided to go to our home. When I tried to open the door, the door was blocked with someone sleeping against it.

A young lady told me the place was packed and I needed to go somewhere else.

I prayed; "Lord, this is too much, what can I do, we are in the street with no money."

A strong thought came to me, "THE LITTLE SISTERS OF JESUS."

I had never met them, but Faithy told me wonderful things about them. Mother Madeleine, the Superior, was the one who created this vocational institution and had received the Pope's benediction.

Mother Madeleine was the one who prayed with Faithy for my conversion.

The Little Sisters of Jesus never closed their door because Jesus said; "I WILL NEVER NO NEVER REJECT ONE OF THEM WHO COMES TO ME." (John 6:37)

They hosted us with pleasure. At the dinner table, Esther fainted. One sister, a doctor, who put Esther in bed, could find nothing serious, except that she was very tired. All the sisters were very efficient. They built themselves a small village, not far from the Vatican. They witnessed their love of Jesus in the streets by their actions, feeding the poor, helping prostitutes, taking care of the homeless. Some of the sisters were educated in engineering, mechanics, carpentry and gardening amongst many other traits.

Mother Madeleine was reading the shopping list.

She said; "You rest and pray. I call."

Yes, it was good that I did not find room to stay in my own home. I had a clear understanding that when we give away everything it is no longer yours.

I enjoyed the serenity of this place with my children. After 4 days of a heavenly entourage, I can sincerely say, if I will not be a mom, I would join the Little Sisters of Jesus with no hesitation.

I also understand why God chose for me the Revolution for Jesus, to open my eyes to teach me the Word of God in action, and what it takes to walk by faith.

No religious pastors or priest of any denomination will dare to accept me the way I was. But Jesus did, because He came for the lost soul.

YOUR PEOPLE SHALL BE VOLUNTEERS IN THE DAY OF YOUR POWER, IN THE BEAUTIES OF HOLINESS. (Psalm 110:3)

It was time to go back to Certaldo, where I was needed. Two big trucks followed me with double the amount of the items that were on the list and the transportation was paid for.

"HOW BEAUTIFUL ARE THE FEET OF THOSE WHO PREACH THE GOSPEL OF PEACE, WHO BRING GLAD TIDING OF GOOD THINGS! "Isaiah 52:7)

Russell had a meeting with Emmanuel's mother the Duchess, as he was renting "LA VOLPE" from her.

She told Russell she was not happy about her son being so involved with the Revolution. She asked Russell to keep an eye on what was going on in the other mansion.

"LA VOLPE" (meaning; the fox) was for guests that came every year hunting fox. The house was huge and needed a lot of T L C. Joshua asked me to move there with the children to stay with my husband and be a witness to him and to come to the mansion every day for worship and Bible study.

Saturday and Sunday were dedicated to evangelizing in Florence on a University campus and at public places.

Russell made fun of me because of my radical lifestyle change, always with my Bible and memorizing verses aloud. Everywhere I went, I had my pocket Bible with me. Russell said he was waiting for me to wake up from "hypnosis." That was what he called my conversion.

One day he was drinking and he insulted me. He said I was a prostitute, first with the show business and now with my Jesus... that he never had a wife. And then he pushed me.

Eric was 3 years old, he ran between me and his father and started to bang his little fist with all his strength on his father's legs and shouted at his father in Italian:

"LASCIA STARE MIA MADRE,
TU SEI BRUTTO E CATTIVO E MIA MADRE È BELLA E GENTILE!

Translation: Leave my mother alone! You are ugly and mean and my mother is beautiful and gentle!

My little boy! My hero!
Russell looked down to him and said; "OK! Ha! This is what you are going to do to me when you grow up?"
Russell left.

Sunday night, I was coming back home with the children, full of joy praising God. I started to tell Russell about what happened on the campus, that after I was translating, a mass of people holding hands praying, they accepted Jesus in their hearts. We came back with six young new coverts guys, to learn more about Jesus and that they were staying at the Babe's ranch.

(The house for the new converts.)

I loved the fact that we had a place to stay for all the new born again Christians. It helped them to feel supported as they got strong in the word so they will be able to learn to stand firm and become a witness; Just like the book of ACTS, we shared everything we possessed. Most of the new converts were destitute.

Russell was drinking and said; "Put the kids in bed."

I came back down from upstairs.

Russell shouted; "You had my children at a public place. I am your husband and you put my name in the dirt! I have enough of you."

He punched me in the face, and then slammed me against the wall. He had an evil look he picked up a big ax in the fireplace and lifted up the ax shouting; "I am going to kill you!"

I yelled; "I REBUKE YOU SATAN IN THE NAME OF JESUS CHRIST! CAME OUT OF HIM!"

Russell's eyes changed......Very slowly he put down the ax, like he came out of a trance.

He said; "You'd better go back to your family because I don't know what I am doing anymore."

Bleeding from the beating, I went in silence in the bedroom where Esther and Eric where sleeping.

The next morning, I tried to get up. I was in a lot of pain. I finally got up and threw up. My vision was foggy. Esther ran to call her father.

When Russell saw me, he was scared, he said; "I am taking you to the hospital because what you have is a trauma of the brain."

I told him; "No, because I have to tell them the truth and they will put you in jail, what will happen to Esther and Eric?"

He said, "You need medical help."

I answered; "The Lord healed me before, He can do it again, just sit and read me something from the Bible."

Russell took the Bible, probably thinking it was better than to go to jail. Without a thought he opened the Bible in the middle and started to read.

ISAIAH 28:1-3 "WOE TO THE CROWN OF PRIDE, TO THE DRUNKARDS OF EPHRAIM,

I had my eyes closed listening, surprised at what he was reading. He continued;

WHOSE GLORIOUS BEAUTY IS A FADING FLOWER

WHICH IS AT THE HEAD OF THE VERDANT VALLEYS,

TO THOSE WHO ARE OVERCOME WITH WINE

BEHOLD, THE LORD HAS A MIGHTY AND STRONG ONE

LIKE A TEMPEST OF HAIL AND A DESTROYING STORM,

LIKE A FLOOD OF MIGHTY WATERS OVERFLOWING,

WHO WILL BRING THEM DOWN TO THE EARTH

WITH HIS HAND. THE CROWN OF PRIDE OF

THE DRUNKARDS OF EPHRAIM WILL BE TRAMPLED UNDERFOOT."

Russell stopped offended; "I am not going to read one more line, that's it."

He stood up, walking back and forth.
It was God speaking to him in the message he just read.

Russell said; "I will not stop drinking! The Italian wine is too good and cheap. I don't want to hear another word about it."

He noticed that I was getting worse, he asked; "What can I do?"

I asked him to go to the mansion and bring back someone to pray.

Russell came back with two young sisters and one brother, and then left the room.

Sarah read john 15:7 "IF YOU ABIDE IN ME, AND MY WORDS ABIDE IN YOU, YOU SHALL ASK WHAT YOU WILL, AND IT SHALL BE DONE UNTO YOU"

They prayed: "Lord according to Your words we ask you to heal Mimi......AMEN."

Jesus never did a long prayer. The pain left me, I opened my eyes and my vision was back. The room felt the warm love of Jesus. I stood up and made lunch for everybody. Russell was watching me.

I told him; "You see Jesus did it again!"

Russell said; "Well! I know you can put a good act."

I told him; "You saw me before and you know what you did to me last night, why are you so blind?"

As days went on, I thought to tell my testimony and brag about my career in show business and show pictures to prove it. I thought that was a good way of witnessing.

The leader named Omar asked me if I was born again.

I was very upset and replied: "What kind of question is that? I am here giving everything and you ask me if I am born again? Who are you to talk to me like that? It was easy for you to leave your Angel of Death motorcycle gang you had nothing to give up except your dirty rags."

Omar said; "You're right, but when I became born again, I had a new life. Washed and purified by the blood of Jesus. I also changed my name.

To be born again:

"OLD THINGS ARE PASSED AWAY ALL THINGS ARE NEW."

You cannot keep one foot in the past and one foot in the Kingdom of God

"AND THOSE WHO ARE IN JESUS CHRIST, HAVE CRUCIFIED THE FLESH." (Galatians 5:24) And "HE WHO LOVES HIS LIFE WILL LOSE IT, AND HE WHO DENIED HIS LIFE IN THIS WORLD WILL KEEP IT FOR ETERNAL LIFE. IF ANYONE SERVES ME, LET HIM FOLLOW ME." (John 12:25-26)

To follow Jesus Christ, you cannot look back."

I answered Him; "Do you ever speak your own mind? Do you always have to quote Bible verses when you talk to people?"

Omar replied: "The word of God is always right. That is the reason we memorize the Bible. We are born again by the renewing of our mind. God is my Father I want to talk like Him."

OUCH! I had introspection, and I burned my pictures and magazines with my photos and articles.

Instead of talking about me, I talk about Jesus.

I choose a new name, Elisabeth, because in Hebrew it means "God's house". It was exactly six months since I had joined the Revolution for Jesus. (Elisabeth in the Bible was 6 months pregnant.)

Chapter 12

BODYGUARD

After Russell had beaten me up, Joshua sent three bodyguards to protect me and the children.

(Thank God Russell never brutalized his children.)

With the excuse that they would help fix up the place and do chores like cutting trees for wood for the fireplace. It was winter and Russell accepted the help of Omar, the leader and the strongest one, Amos a Hungarian and Cush a Chinese. In exchange Russell would teach them Italian and feed them. Those three were very active in everything they did. Always reciting Bible verses and praising God with songs.

My job as a public relations person was to provide for all the needs of people in the Revolution and to translate for Joshua with the official people of the town.

Joshua said; "Because of what happened with Russell last Sunday, it will be better for you not to go this Sunday witnessing this time, because your three Bodyguards will not be back until Monday evening. We have brothers who have memorized salvation verses and songs in Italian. They are confident that the Holy Spirit will give them the knowledge they need to witness, but of course they will not be able to answer people's questions.

I told him: "Jesus said; "BLESSED ARE YOU WHEN THEY REVILE AND PERSECUTE YOU AND SAY ALL KINDS OF EVIL AGAINST YOU

FALSELY FOR MY SAKE. REJOICE AND BE EXCEEDINGLY GLAD FOR GREAT IS YOUR REWARD IN HEAVEN!" I am going, I am blessed."

Sunday evening coming back from witnessing, it was a dark cold night. Before going to LA VOLPE, on the top of the hill, a black cloud of fear gripped my heart. Esther and Eric were sleeping in the back seat of the car.

The deserted environment suddenly looked gloomy. I refused to fall in it, and I started to sing very loudly.

CHEER UP SAINT OF GOD,

IS NOTHING TO WORRY ABOUT,

NOTHING TO MAKE YOU FEEL AFRAID,

NOTHING TO MAKE YOU DOUBT,

OUR GOD NEVER FAILS,

SO WHY NOT TRUST HIM AND,

SHOUT!!!! HALLELUIA! HALLELUIA! HALLELUIA!

I pushed down on the accelerator pedal and arrived in the front of the main entrance. Russell was sober and painting.

Thursday night, Russell came back from Firenze at 2 am, very drunk and mean. He started to argue with Omar. The three young men had been sleeping in the family room near the fireplace. Omar let Russell argue and push him and said nothing. But when Russell went after Cush and Amos, Omar Jumped up and told him not to put one finger on his guys.

Omar was powerful; he put himself in front of them ready to protect them. Russell realized that Omar was stronger than him. He turned around and went upstairs.

Russell in rage kicked the door of the bedroom, where I was with Esther and Eric. The children were sleeping. He then kicked the small electric heater, a little carpet started to burn. I grabbed the carpet, opened the window and threw it out.

I begged him not to wake up the children and to get out of the room.

He started to physically fight me. I was fighting back and tried to kick him in his privates, but Russell caught my foot with one hand and grabbed my throat with his other hand, he lifted me up to the top of his head like I was a feather.

Russell said; "I am going to throw you out the window!!"

That old house was very high; the window was at least 40 feet up from the stony ground.

I closed my eyes and in a desperate prayer I said; "LORD HELP!" And instead of going out the window I fell on the bed. I opened up my eyes to see Russell against the wall sliding down on the floor, blood coming out of his mouth. Then I saw a foot kicking him in the face.

I screamed; "No please! That's enough!"

I saw Omar and Cush standing there, my body guards. Omar had saved my life.

I remembered the message Russell was reading in (Isaiah 28) "THE CROWN OF PRIDE OF THE DRUNKARD SHALL BE TRODDEN UNDER FEET."

Omar and Cush took me and the children to the main mansion to take refuge. Omar reported to Joshua and went back to take care of Russell with a first aid kit. He stayed with him and witnessed to him, but Russell refused to stop drinking and left the country.

Russell was gone, I was free, to dedicate all my time to the Revolution for Jesus.

We used LA VOLPE, to host the new Italian converts.

I was the spiritual mother of 70 new converts. Omar was teaching the men and Joshua was the head of mature Christians.

We had a separate home dedicated to the young pregnant women, so they would not go through with having abortions. We took care of them to have their babies and had a midwife from the near village come to assist them when the time came. The midwife was amazed to see these young women not complaining or screaming but instead cry out "halleluiah!" while giving birth to healthy babies despite of past drug addictions. What a testimony for everyone. Glory to God! Thank You Jesus!

I found myself running in so many directions because of all the tremendous needs of so many.

I had to leave my children with a girl in charge of the nursery. Day after day things were getting worse in my eyes.

Esther and Eric were very affectionate and well behaved. They never complained, they shared everything they had with other kids. Never asked for anything and always thankful for whatever they had.

One day coming back from errands, I found Esther and Eric covered with lice. I freaked out.

After I told Omar, he gave me a serious look and said; "Elisabeth (my new name), if a few small insects can make you so upset, you'd better quit now because in the Revolution for Jesus you must expect much worse than lice."

OUCH! That guy really put me in my place.

A few days later, I came back from provisioning to find my five-year-old Esther, in tears. She told me the girl Leha, a 24-year-old American girl who was in charge of the nursery, forced her to pick up poop from the floor from a toddler with her bare hands and put it in the toilet.

I was furious! Not only was I providing everything for everybody but now my children were taught to do things I was not ok with, NO way! I asked the girl what was wrong with her.

She was laughing and said; "There is nothing wrong with poop, it is digested food, Esther must learn about the real value of life!"

I went to talk to Faithy who just came to do an inspection and to see what was going on.

She said; "Those young people used to be so wasted with heavy drugs. It is a real miracle the way they are compared to a year ago; we need to be patient and loving."

I did not get over it. And then to see my children sleeping on the floor with a small blanket because they took Esther and Eric's bed to give to their own children.

That was it! My children were more important to me than all those people. I took them with me in my room and started to pack a bag.

That night I prayed; "Lord thank you for all the teachings, now I know You Lord and I am strong in faith, I can go back to Rome, in show business and witness to all those lost souls and help the poor."

Exhausted, I fell asleep. I dreamt I was back on stage all my admirers were giving me flowers and jewelry. As I lifted my arm to admire the big precious stone on my ring finger, my hand started to change color slowly; it became dry and black going up to my arm and my neck. That thing was going up to my face! I screamed and then woke up. Trembling, I opened my Bible and this scripture was jumping out of the page at me; (John 15:6)

"IF ANYONE DOES NOT ABIDE IN ME, HE IS CAST OUT AS A BRANCH, AND IS WITHERED AND THEY GATHER THEM, AND THROW THEM INTO THE FIRE, AND THEY ARE BURNED." (John 15:6)

WOW! Oh no! I remembered my death experience in 1969.

I shared my concern about my children to Omar. Right away, he spoke with the head leader. He asked him to let him be in charge of my children. The request was granted, Omar would be in charge.

Omar Often would take Eric with him when he was repairing cars or other stuff, telling him to pass him the tools, teaching him to be a man of God and the importance to be a child of the King.

When Omar went witnessing, he would put Esther on his shoulders and tell her to translate in Italian for him. He was a good father figure and the children started to be much happier to feel needed and participating for winning souls.

They memorized; PSALM 112:1 "PRAISE THE LORD! BLESSED IS THE MAN WHO FEARS THE LORD, WHO DELIGHTS GREATLY IN HIS COMMANDMENTS"

They sang in Italian at public places, Esther playing on her small guitar, she was almost 6 years old;

"YOU GOT TO BE A BABY TO GO TO HEAVEN! JESUS SAID; LET THE LITTLE CHILDREN COME TO ME"

They both distributed free salvation literature. Nobody ever says no to children. They were a huge blessing to everybody.

The head leaders noticed the excellent job Omar and I were doing as a team. After almost a year, we had a meeting with the elders. They said Omar was an excellent father to my children and that it was time for me to marry Omar.

I asked; "But what about Russell?"

They answered; "The Bible said, if a nonbeliever leaves, you are free to be remarried. We will give you our blessing so you can go together on the mission field,"

I was asking more questions about the ethics, but they replied: "That is the way it was done in the Bible, which is the way we will do it too."

Everybody loved and admired Omar, and I did too. His life was a good example for everyone.

In the winter, I saw him give his only coat to a new convert who was cold.

He had visions and prophesied all the time. He had been chosen as a leader after the Holy Spirit came in the form of a tongue of fire coming upon his head. He was firm in his faith and learned to depend on God for direction.

One night, I had a vision of a big gold crown suspended in the sky, and the voice of my mother screaming about me; "She is dead because she saw God!"

Then the voice of the Lord said; "Your crown is waiting for you!"

A few days later, I had another vision. I saw an enormous tree, and a multitude of all kinds of birds come to take refuge in it, but most of them were black birds. I asked the Lord what it means...

The Lord revealed to me that I was the tree and the black birds were the ones rejected by formal churches and that he wanted me to minister to them.

For months God strengthened my soul with dreams and visions, to prepare me for a difficult time.

There was a big need in India and we learned about all the wonderful things Mother Theresa was doing there. The leaders decided that Omar, me and the children should go there.

We needed a good transportation. I told them I had a car in Rome in a friend's garage. My friend had not sold it because he said I would come back to ask for it one day.

The Alfa Romeo 2600 was, for Omar, a dream engine. He examined everything and said it would be a good thing to sell it and buy something less luxurious, but after he drove it, he fell in love with the powerful motor and the comfortable seat and the large space in the back for Esther and Eric. But that was not a car for missionary work.

We hit the road, direction south of France. Omar was a very good driver, he had never had any accidents in the Revolution, but he got distracted watching all those different speedometers on the dashboard and did not notice the two cars in front of us stopping to make a left turn. He ran into the car in front of him, which propelled him to hit the car in front of him. None of us or the other car passengers got hurt, thank God, but we damaged two cars.

Our front frame went into the left tire, we were not able to continue our trip until the car could be fixed. Omar was devastated to cause an accident. And being a leader in the Revolution, there were consequences. They forbid anyone who had an accident, if at fault or not, to drive for six months. This was because it was proof one did not pray and ask God for protection before starting the car. We are supposed to pray at all times, for everything.

Omar said; "But I did pray! I think it was God wanting to stop us. It is probably not His will for us to go to India with the children and you pregnant."

Omar was the leader and he heard the voice of the Lord, so I agreed with everything he said.

He asked the garage owner to let him fix the cars because we were short on money. The man accepted and he offered Omar a job as a mechanic.

Omar called his mother, Magda. She was the director of the financing department in a hospital in Montreal in Canada. He explained to her the situation.

She listened her 24 years old son, telling her he was expecting a child with a 34 years old French woman, which had two toddlers from another marriage.

She told him we must come to Montreal to have the baby since some of the best gynecologists and surgeons worked in this hospital and had good success with this new epidural anesthesia. Omar explained to her, I needed a third C-section and my problems with anesthesia in my previous births.

A few weeks later, I had a vision. I was in a boat alone with my children, in the Ocean, in the midst of a tempest, standing up with a large coat with my arms open, covering my children from the storm, like a hen covering her babies under her wings.

I was disturbed by this vision, to be pregnant and to cross the Ocean, also the apprehension to meet Omar's mother. Omar said I was probably affected and in fear because of my last C-section.

Chapter 13

MONTREAL

Omar's mother and her husband were so happy to have their son back. Magda was thankful for me because her son would not have come home if it were not for my condition.

After a couple of weeks Omar found a job at a printing office and we moved out of his mom's house. We rented an apartment.

The day arrived, February 11, 1974.

I was reciting Psalm 121 on the way to the operation table.

I WILL LIFT UP MY EYES TO THE HILLS

FROM WHENCE COMETH MY HELP

MY HELP COMETH FROM THE LORD,

WHO MADE HEAVEN AND EARTH.

HE WILL NOT ALLOW MY FOOT TO BE MOVED,

HE WHO KEEPS ME WILL NOT SLUMBER.

Even though doctor Bruyere was agnostic, he never made a negative comment about God. He just smiled and kept a steady conversation during surgery.

Suddenly he exclaimed; "She is full of tumors I have to clean her up before I can take the baby out."

He started to cut away at the tumors.

I told him; "You see, God left them in me for you to see, because you did not believe me, when I told you that God healed me in 1972. By God's grace, they have been inactive."

I remembered about two years earlier in my Art Gallery in Rome; I was sitting in the Bible study with a Group of believers and one young lady said to me;

"Mimi, the Lord just told me that you are going to have another child."

I told her; "No way, that is impossible. I cannot have another child. My insides are a mess and the doctor told me I could never have another child because of what I did to my body."

I did not know about Omar's existence then and I was not walking by spiritual faith in those days.

She smiled and said; "You will see, with God all things are possible!"

The surgery was taking more time than planned because of the removal of tumors and the epidural was starting to wear off. I started to have excruciating pain.

The surgeon said; "Please hang on! Just one minute and the baby will be out."

The nurse was ready next to me with a syringe, to inject me as soon as the baby would be out.

For the first time, I was able to witness the birth of one of my babies before closing my eyes.

When I woke up, a nurse asked me what would be the baby's name.

I told her; "Her name is Anne Elisabeth, Anne meaning GRACE and Elisabeth, GOD'S HOUSE."

The nurse's face turned red she was very upset. I realized I was in the French section of Montreal. The English and the French were still having a ridiculous cold war. The name I just gave my baby was the name of Princess Anne and Queen Elisabeth of England.

Omar's mother was from Hungarian and Russian blood lines, and named her Anouchka and later on we call her Nouchka. She was a very good baby. Always smiled and laughed.

My recovery was very slow. My seven years old Esther was acting like a little mother. She prepared breakfast and looked after Eric, me and Nouchka. Eric was five years old and did more than a boy his age could do. He was very quiet and made sure that I would have to walk only the minimum by putting in my hands the things I needed to take care of baby Nouchka.

Omar, unfortunately, not only worked in the printer shop but his mother wanted him to work for her doing paper work. She said she needed his help and he needed extra money.

In this particular time, I would appreciate it if he would be home instead of spending every Friday to Sunday away from home. Omar was neglecting also his time with God. I started to observe Omar returning in the flesh, he became irritated if I asked where he was.

I had a nightmare. I dreamt that my bed was full of snakes. I woke up in sweat, with a bad feeling.

Omar called from his mother's home. He said; "I have the results from your last test. The doctor told me the cancerous tumors have spread all over, he cannot operate on you, and you don't have much time to live anymore."

I told him; "I rebuke this statement! Where is your faith? God healed me before HE WILL do it again. God did not give me another baby to have three orphans. Come on Omar let's go back on the road and win souls for the King!"

Omar replied; "You are sick! You cannot do that. I don't want to be in the Revolution for Jesus anymore! I am young. I want to start a new life for myself; I cannot be stuck with three children. I want you to go back to your family in France, you can leave Nouchka here, I will put her up for adoption. I want you to know I am back with my old girlfriend."

I was listening in silence, my heart was breaking, that was the man of God I thought I knew talking to me? Abandoned me and the children at the worst time of my life? The phone fell out of my hands; I fell on my knees, my head exploding with a hundred questions. It was like a knife penetrating in my chest and stabbing me over and over until I could not breathe anymore.

I was asking God WHY?

I was talking to God; "Your words, said" you know everything, the present, the future, if that is so, why did You let this happen? My children are innocent; do I deserve punishment for loving Omar too much and listening to him instead of You? I thought that's what the women in the Bible are supposed to do, but if You are the God that loved and forgave even David, why do you punish my children? If You are a good God, if You love the world full of sin for which Your only Son died for, what about me? The pain is too big to bear, my flesh is consumed with cancer and there is no one to help me, I am abandoned, like a piece of trash. Where are you God? Why are You so mean to me and my little ones?"

I heard a voice inside my head; "AN ENEMY OF GOD DID THAT TO YOU."

The Bible had fallen on the floor with me and the page was open to Isaiah 54:4-6, my tears were falling on the verses as I started to read.

DO NOT FEAR FOR YOU WILL NOT BE ASHAMED

NOR BE DISGRACED

FOR YOU WILL FORGET THE SHAME OF YOUR YOUTH.

FOR YOUR MAKER IS YOUR HUSBAND,

THE LORD OF HOSTS IS HIS NAME,

YOUR REDEEMER IS THE HOLY ONE OF ISRAEL.

HE IS CALLED THE GOD OF THE WHOLE EARTH.

FOR THE LORD HAS CALLED YOU

LIKE A WOMAN FORSAKEN AND GRIEVED IN THE SPIRIT,

LIKE A YOUTHFUL WIFE WHEN YOU WERE REFUSED.

SAYS YOUR GOD."

The pain became numbness. God used the Bible to fall on the floor and open to Isaiah 54:4-6, which spoke directly to my heart, every word penetrated inside my soul to comfort me. If The God of the entire Universe said; He was my HUSBAND! That was the best revelation I could have.

I worshipped Him, and surrendered all to Him.

"I LOVE THE LORD BECAUSE HE HAS HEARD MY VOICE AND MY SUPPLICATIONS. BECAUSE HE HAS INCLINED HIS EAR UNTO ME, THEREFORE I WILL CALL UPON HIM AS LONG AS I LIVE. (Psalm 116:1-2)

Chapter 14

BACK TO EUROPE

It was very hard. Esther and Eric did not understand why we had to go back to Europe. To leave their friends, school, all their toys and belongings and worst of all, the man they thought was their father. Nouchka was only 4 months old and did not know anything; the most important thing for her was to be near her mom's breast. To grow up with no father was very hard for all of my 3 children.

I went to Geneva, Switzerland, because I did not want to be a burden for my parents.

I started working as a governess for a Christian couple from Finland. The husband was the treasurer for the United Nations. The couples were having problems with their two teenage girls. I was not too old to communicate with teenagers and not too young to understand their parents' concerns. I became the bridge.

I was depending on God's grace to have strength for each day. It was God's blessing that I was accepted with my children with so much love as a part of the family. After two months, the children reconnected with their parents.

The American leader of the Revolution for Jesus in Geneva told me he was praying for a French speaking missionary to pioneer the south of France and said;

"Praise God! And here you are."

He gave me two young American couples with two small children to teach them French. They were supposed to help me but unfortunately, they were more a burden than help.

In France, I continued witnessing with baby Nouchka on my baby backpack.

Esther and Eric distributed literature about salvation. We met a lot of people. In less than a month, God opened the door of a big villa, 10 miles out of Montpellier.

That was the first shelter in the south of France for the Revolution for Jesus.

Eric was often asking; "When will dad come back? I want dad to be here with us."

We prayed every day for Omar to come back to serve God.

One day the phone rang at the new shelter and it was Omar. He asked if I could send him the money for a plane ticket so he could come back to serve God.

We leaped in joy.

The only income we had was from the government check, and donations made to our organization.

To be able to send money for a plane ticket to Omar, I had to have a meeting with the other leaders. They said that I could not use my children's government income (In 1975, in France, the government pays a woman with 3 children about 1200 dollars a month as a assistance.)

That was our rent money. Jason, one of the leaders who insisted on being in charge of the treasurer, made lots of mistakes. The fund was not only empty, but we did not have enough to pay the rent.

I was giving everything I had, and I wanted to send money to Omar. I started to do double shifts on the road, with Nouchka, four months old.

I had Nouchka on my back and breastfeeding her every four hours, while Esther and Eric helped distribute literature.

After a vote, I was put in charge of the finances and very soon things changed, the rent was paid and there was money in the treasury.

Omar used to be such a big help for the Revolution, he was very much needed plus he was fluent in French.

I went on the road every day with the children filled with joy, saving every penny, depriving ourselves from food and transportation, hitch hiking etc.

I never asked myself why I needed to do that, he had a good job and a wealthy mother. He did not need us to pay for his plane ticket.

Chapter 15

DOUBLE BETRAYAL

After I sent him the money, Omar called and said; "I must tell you, do not wait for me to come back, I am getting married, I release you from your vow. I am sure there are many guys in the Revolution that would love to marry you."

Omar said more things, but I dropped the phone in disbelief.

It was so hard to face Esther and Eric, waiting for good news with big smiles on their faces. I was not able to hold back my tears. They tried their best to be courageous.

My seven years old daughter Esther, asked; "Why, since we serve Jesus, why did Jesus who can do everything let this happen? I thought Jesus loved me, but I don't see it, we gave everything to him. Why can't I have a dad like the other children? Jesus! I don't love you anymore!"

Esther and Eric in my arms, we cried in silence, baby Nouchka was sleeping.

I whispered in their ears; "God is the only father that will always be with you"

Eric crying said; "God is too big, I cannot hug Him, He is too big for me! I just want my dad to hold me."

PSALM 119:156 GREAT ARE YOUR MERCIES O LORD REVIVE ME ACCORDING TO YOUR JUDGMENTS.

About a month later, I was sent to pioneer further in the south of France. Jason called for a meeting, telling me since I had filled up the villa with a new bunch of spiritual babes; I had to go pioneering somewhere else to find new territory and had to leave behind Esther and Eric and take only baby Nouchka who needed to be breastfed. Jason was watching me expecting me to blow up. But to his surprise, I told him about the dream I had last night.

Jesus was asking me; "DO YOU LOVE ME MORE THAN YOUR CHILDREN?"

I was so beat up already, that was so hard to answer; I was living every day for my children with my eyes on Jesus to give me strength.

They needed me more than Jesus, but on the other hand, I recognized that if it would not be for Jesus, my children would be orphans a long time ago.

Jason and his wife, with their two little children and two French Christian girls, would be taking care of them.

I was sent to Perpignan, a nice historic town in the south of France. I had with me; two French speaking converts Phillip an English brother. I was completely depending on God's grace. We ministered to the owner of a hotel and he gave us a room in exchange for doing some cleaning.

After we won a few souls, the room became too small for us as we were adding sleeping bags like sardines in a can.

We found another place with a bigger room. Now we were twelve people sleeping on the floor except for me and Nouchka on a bed since I was the leader and the older, plus with a baby.

We made lots of friends and lots of enemies. One morning during devotion and Bible reading, somebody opened the door quickly and threw a small explosive into the room.

Everybody jumped up; some went through the window (we were on the first floor). I, with Nouchka in my arms, fell on the back of a piece of furniture all the while covering her with my body. A lot of smoke. We had bruises, but nothing serious. It was time for us to move out.

Phillip, our English brother, my assistant leader, came back with good news. An old man had put a house for sale and would let us use it until he found a buyer.

I always wore clean khakis or jeans with a nice clean shirt. I never looked like a hippie. Every day I went out witnessing in public places to a bunch of hippies. It was the seventies... One day, an aggressive young man wanted to hurt me, just after I distributed croissants, he started insulting me. Two young guys protected me and took him away.

In the evening, at dinner time, everybody was back with exciting reports from their witnessing encounters.

Phillip arrived with a black eye and blood on his lips.

I asked him "What happened?"

Phillip said; "It was worth it",

The same guy who tried to assault me followed him inside.

The guy was very embarrassed when he saw me, but I just opened my arms and welcomed him for dinner. Everybody was sitting on the floor.

I had a big pot of green beans with little pieces of meat. I served everyone a big ladle. We also had a huge basket of fruit donated from the market place.

The new comer explained what had happened that afternoon.

He said; "When Phillip talked to me about Jesus, I punched him two times in the face very hard and Phillip, instead of going away, got up and gave me his other cheek to punch, and said;

"Jesus loves you and I love you too."

I said to him; "what kind of a nut are you?"

And Phillip replied; "The kind that loves Jesus enough, to live or die for Him, to tell you about eternal life and heaven so you will not burn in hell for eternity."

So that was what he did, and prayed for me, and I felt something deep inside...and I accepted Jesus."

We all celebrated, praising God with singing and dancing.

PSALM 150:4 PRAISE THE LORD WITH THE TIMBREL AND DANCE... LET EVERYTHING THAT HATH BREATH PRAISE THE LORD!

I wanted to see my children, my heart was heavy, I prayed;

"Please Lord only you can make it happen, send someone to drive me to Montpellier."

The next morning, very early, someone entered the room to wake me up with Nouchka...waking everyone as well who were sleeping on the floor in sleeping bags.
That was Louis Bousquet, an architect who was an important man in the town of Perpignan.

Louis said: "Elisabeth! Get ready with Nouchka, I have a meeting in Montpellier and I will take you to visit Esther and Eric."

I jumped out of bed screaming "THANK YOU JESUS!"

Louis said with a smile: "My name is Louis not Jesus."

Louis explained that he woke up in the middle of the night and was not able to sleep. Something told him that Esther and Eric missed their mom and he was able to help.

I met Louis about five months earlier when I first came to Perpignan with my three children on a faith trip to inspect for the right town to pioneer and establish another refuge to win lost souls.

I met Louis in the street in Perpignan. Louis was an agnostic. When I offered him a salvation pamphlet, he refused it and with a hostile tone in his voice he said a few ugly words and walked away.

I said to him; "Jesus loves you and we do too."

About 20 minutes later, he came back, and invited me with my three children to his home to meet his wife Michelle, and their two teenage children. Little Esther played her guitar and witnessed in song, which made a huge impression on the family. Immediately their boy and their girl picked up their guitar and asked Esther to teach them the song.

They hosted us for a week and blessed us with comfort, asking lots of questions about my faith, and what happened to me to be by myself with three children on the road talking about Jesus.

Since that day we stayed in contact. His wife, Michelle, was a social worker before she married Louis. She felt it was time for her to go back to her job, helping people.

They did not believe that religion could do much for people compared to government social services.

In Montpellier, Esther and Eric looked so pale and skinny. They were malnourished and suffered from the separation from their mom.

I had a talk with Jason telling him: "I am taking my children with me."

He refused vehemently, and said: "I am the leader now and you must submit to my authority, like the Bible says!"

It was so hard to tell Esther and Eric: "I will come back we need to pray for God to make a way.

PSALM 119:121 I HAVE DONE JUSTICE AND RIGHTEOUSNESS LORD DO NOT LEAVE ME TO MY OPPRESSORS.

About two weeks later in Perpignan, I took Nouchka on my backpack along with a new convert and went on the road to teach him how to walk by faith. I told him we are going to hitchhike to Montpellier. This new convert had a very scary look; he was tall and large with a very rough face and long hair with a bandana like an Indian.

That was not the style in 1975. People made detours around him, which seemed to make him more aggressive. The first time I witnessed to him, he was sitting on the ground baby Nouchka, one year old, walked over to him and put her arms around his neck and gave him a big kiss. I wished someone would have filmed it, the guy completely melted and from that moment, he became our bodyguard. I called him "Savate souriante," which means "Smiling slippers," because his shoe was broken in the front and you could see his toes.

When I told him we were going to be hitchhiking.

He said: "You will never get a ride with my looks; no one is going to stop."

I told him if God wanted me to go see my children, He would provide the ride. Montpellier was about 200 miles away. We walked a half mile towards the highway, and stopped so I could feed Nouchka just a little way from the road and sat on the grass.

"Savate souriante" stood on the road, looking around. A car stopped next to him and the driver asked him if he needed a ride. He did not even have his thumb out. He was so shocked he could hardly say a word.

The driver brought us right to the center of Montpellier.

We went first to see a couple, Charles and Ginette Giral, who owned a small restaurant. They had been very fond of me and Ginette was a charismatic Christian she was very sensitive to the Holy Spirit. The Revolution for Jesus refuge was about 10 miles out of town.

Ginette said; "Come sit, eat and relax. When we close the restaurant, Charles will drive you to the villa and "Savate souriante" will help me clean up the place. Charles will make Jason release the children to you. We know that Jason just wanted to keep Esther and Eric in hostage so he could continue to collect government money from the children."

When we arrived at the villa, I noticed the car belonging to Timothy, the head leader from Marseille, was parked there. I asked Jason if I could talk to him, but Jason said he was not there. I asked him to see my children.

Jason said: "No, they are sleeping you must come back tomorrow."

I could feel he wanted me out quickly. Charles Giral was a head taller than Jason and very authoritarian. He ordered him to let me see my children right away.

Eric, who slept on the top of the bunk bed, was sick with fever. He opened his eyes, hugged me and cried silently on my shoulder.

Esther got up from her bed and said: "If you would have not come, we would have run away. Jason is mean and stole the package that Grandpa sent us with chocolates and then he ate them in the front of us and said mmm, it's so good but not for children."

Eric said: "Last night I cried and prayed, please Lord I want my mom! And God did it!"

I asked the girls why they had not called the doctor for Eric.

They answered: "We prayed for Eric to be healed a week ago and he said he was healed."

I needed the love of God for not punching those people in the face. Eric was five years old, and probably scared to disagree with them.

I went out of the room. Charles was with the children to prepare them to leave with us.

I closed my eyes in prayer to ask God to help me.

A door opened and there was Timothy, we hugged each other. And I told him about the situation. Timothy was surprised; he said that Jason told him I did not want my children when I am pioneering.

I started to cry exhausted and told him Jason keeps my children in hostage in order to get my government money. I want my children; they are sick, skinny, not well fed, not taken good care of. When I called Jason, he would not let me talk to them. He has forgotten where he came from. He is cruel to my children and to his own child. I had enough; I am out of the Revolution. That is not the way to serve God.

Charles and I came back with the children to the Giral home. They called their doctor who put Eric on antibiotics. Esther had the same virus, but she was taken care of in time and was better in three days.

During that time "Savate souriante" was cleaning the restaurant kitchen. A customer gave him a ride back to Perpignan.

After a week, it was time to go back to Perpignan. We got a ride also from one customer of the restaurant.

Eric was pale and weak throwing up often. He never complained. He was happy just to be with his mother again.

PSALM 120:1-2 IN MY DISTRESS I CRIED TO THE LORD
AND HE HEARD ME DELIVER MY SOUL O LORD FROM
LYING LIPS AND FROM A DECEITFUL TONGUE.

Chapter 16

TRAITOR IN THE MIDST

When we arrived in Perpignan, another surprise was waiting for me. A young Frenchman named Mark had taken the leadership by force.

He said; "Being in France, we need French leaders. Not like the Englishman or Americans... Since Elisabeth is gone, I am in charge."

Mark was a very new convert with only about seven months in the Revolution. He used to be with the New Age type of worship, which is a shadow of spirituality searching for self-esteem and balance of the spirit, body and mind. Their goal is to be enlightened and empowered, and they claim to be gods and goddesses. Using Bible verses.

Mark used to say: "I don't need a church I am a very spiritual person."

Mark was very involved in Indian meditation, astrology, yoga and anything to prove he did not need Jesus.

He first came to the Revolution to prove to us that what he had was more powerful than the Holy Spirit.

One day his eyes were fixed on a piece of paper on the table during lunch and the paper started burning.

Mark exclaimed: "My spirit world can do what you cannot do!"

I answered him: "My Spirit world is Holy and He can do what your spirit cannot do! By the power of the blood of Jesus Christ, by the authority of the name above all names, Jesus the Son of God, I command you Satan to come out of him NOW!"

Mark accepted Jesus and walked with the Lord for about seven months.

When I was his leader, he was very nice to me. Maybe he was too nice. After he became aware that his courting was going nowhere, he used the time I was gone to take over.

I asked him: "Where are Phillip and all the new converts from last month?"

He replied: "I sent them on the road to pioneer new territory. I don't want needy people in my camp, I am targeting only the rich and I don't want children, I'm in charge now."

I was so sad that there were so many rotten apples in the basket of those who called themselves Children of God.

Walking slowly in the street with my three children, we stopped at a crepes restaurant to eat.

The owner of the restaurant asked Esther if she could play something on her guitar for her. Esther always carried her guitar wherever she went. That was her companion. She was always ready to please. Singing was how she coped, that was her therapy. She started to sing (in French) a bible verse about children.

MATTHEW 18:3 JESUS SAID, UNLESS YOU ARE CONVERTED AND BECOME AS LITTLE CHILDREN YOU WILL BY NO MEANS ENTER THE KINGDOM OF HEAVEN.

The young lady asked: "where do you live?"

I told her; "God will provide a place for us."

A few minutes later, a couple came inside. After the owner talked to them, they started to walk out but then turned back around and said to her: "OK, we will take them home with us."

They were the parents of the lady that owned the restaurant. They hosted us.

A few days later, somebody gave baby Nouchka some cherries that were not washed and had a new pesticide on it. Many got sick from it.

Nouchka got so sick, almost to the point of death. Antibiotics did not work. Everything she ate or drank went out of her as fast as it got inside her mouth. The doctor told me to bring her to the hospital.

The nurses took Nouchka from my arms and put her inside a glass room with no access to anyone except the medical staff. Every day, I went to see her through the glass window.

In between visits, I went with Esther and Eric witnessing in the streets of Perpignan, giving out pamphlets.

One police atheist woman arrested me when she found out that I did not have a home and a job with income.

The Police called social services and took Esther and Eric away from me. They told me I can have my children back only after I have a job and a F 3 apartment.

Nouchka was in the hospital and Esther and Eric in an orphanage shelter.

With the help of the couple who had hosted us, I got a job as a waitress in a restaurant on the beach at Saint Cyprien.

Saint Cyprien was a small tourist town very busy during summer. A studio was included with the job.

After a week, early morning I called the Bousquet. Louis answered and said they had just come back from their June vacation.

I explained to him what had happened to us, that social services wanted me to have a three bedrooms apartment before I can have my children back and I now was in a studio.

Louis was mad; "I am going to make some phone calls and make sure you can have Esther and Eric back with you today!"

Louis came to pick me up and take back the children from the orphanage shelter.

Esther and Eric said it was worse than being with Jason, nobody prayed and everyone fought

.

Eric said: "I had to put my pillow on top of my head so I would not feel the pain of the beatings, I refused to cry, I did not want to make Satan happy."

I prepared a space for Esther and Eric. They would play in the back yard until I finished work.

I was on my knees every day in supplication asking God in the name of Jesus Christ to heal Nouchka. She was not responding to any treatment she was only getting worse.

One morning I was agonizing begging God for Nouchka, suddenly I visualized life with Jesus, no more pain no more needs, no more tears, just perfect peace and joy forever.

No one could hurt you anymore. I realized if I loved my child that much, then I wanted what was the best for her. I did not have anything to offer her.

I prayed; "Lord, you can take Nouchka, she will be so happy with you, please forgive me for being so selfish to want her to be with me in this troubled world, but Lord in your mercy please take the pain away. I love You Lord."

I went early morning in the hospital like my daily routine. The doctor was in the hallway.

He said to me; "Good morning, Madame Hinman (my last name) this morning I was surprised to find your child in good shape. I guess our treatment and the mashed carrot soup got her well faster than expected. You can take her home with you today."

I was Glorifying God! I knew it was the Lord who did it!

The scripture about Abraham offering his son Isaac to God came immediately in my remembrance. God wanted to know if Abraham loved Him more than his son. Many say that God planned everything about us and our future, if that is so, why did God want to know if Abraham loved him more than his son?

The Bible repeatedly says: "If you are faithful, if you obey my commandments, if you don't turn away from me... I will watch over you and protect you."

Some are questioning why God asked Abraham to kill his son. In those days, in the culture Abraham lived, a multitude of people were worshipers of idols and they would offer to their gods their first child.

God wanted to know if Abraham loved Him as much as those idol worshippers.

GENESIS 22:11-12 BUT THE ANGEL OF THE LORD, CALLED TO HIM FROM HEAVEN AND SAID ABRAHAM AND HE SAID; HERE I AM, AND HE SAID TO HIM; DO NOT LAY YOUR HAND ON THE LAD, OR DO ANYTHING TO HIM, FOR NOW I KNOW THAT YOU FEAR GOD SINCE YOU HAVE NOT WITH HELD YOUR ONLY SON FROM ME.

I was not able to stop praising and giving thanks to my Lord.

THE LORD SPOKE TO ME; "IF YOU STAY FAITHFUL AND DO WHAT I COMMAND YOU TO DO, YOU WILL BE WITH ME, I ALREADY PREPARED A PLACE FOR YOU. DON'T LOOK TO OTHERS FOR GRATIFICATION BUT LOOK TO ME, STAND FIRM AGAINST THE ENEMY OF YOUR SOUL, FEAR NOT I WILL HOLD YOUR HAND, BE

COURAGEOUS YOU ARE NOT ALONE, I AM ALWAYS WITH YOU, DON'T LOSE YOUR CROWN."

This means it is up to us to stay faithful. Satan is the seducer and the prince of this world. He tries to attract us with temptations to destroy us. It is a real war in the Spirit.

Esther seven and Eric, five years old, were taking care of Nouchka when I was working.

Chapter 17

THE MADAME

The owner of the restaurant was some type of "Madame". She had some customers who came to her to find easy girls.

I was the only waitress doing the job of two. I never complained and I prayed continually, happy to have my children with me again.

When a customer would ask me to sit at their table, I had the opportunity to speak with passion about love, telling them the real love they needed was Jesus Christ.

The Madame told me not to do that, but her husband would often listen in. He called me "Holy Elisabeth."

Sometimes their daughter came to sit at the table with me with a few clients,

she said to me; "Don't you feel ashamed to always talk about Jesus? that is a personal matter."

I answered her; "I would be more ashamed if Jesus was to be ashamed of me for not being faithful to him."

Madame was furious but was not able to find anyone to replace me. One day she was really evil possessed. She did not want me to go feed my children during the break, at which time the restaurant was closed, 3 pm until 4pm.

I refused, she said I needed to have someone to take care of my children, because she needed me in the restaurant extra hours for cleaning. The same day I called my mother who lived in the east of France about 500 miles away.

I told her, mom I never asked you for anything, but please I need you to come here for at least one week. I explained our situation, with the social service taking my children away.

My mom told me she will take the first train the next day and will arrive in the afternoon for me to pick her up.

After this long trip, I installed my 64year- old mom in my bed to relax, the children took a nap, and I went back to work.

The next day at 3 pm, I took my lunch break and ran over to see my family. The home was empty, no sign of my family or of our belongings.

I ran back to the restaurant and asked the Madame what she had done with my family.

She said she put them in the public trailer park because she needed the studio until she could find a waitress more suitable to her.

I found my mother in tears she said, she would not stay one more day with the children in this trailer full of mice.

I went back to talk to the Madame and asked her to respect her oral contract that included the studio.

She refused vehemently. The policeman inspector had just arrived as he was one of our regular customers. He came to the restaurant every evening and always wanted me to serve him to have conversation.

She wanted me to go to take his order, I said; "No, not unless you give me back the studio and let me be with my family, if not, I want you to pay me right now for the last two weeks I worked here."

She started to argue but then she watched the inspector looking in our direction.

The inspector noticed that something was going on. He got up and started walking in our direction.

The Madame suddenly agreed to pay me, grumbling about her having to do my job.

I thanked her, said goodbye to her husband and the policeman and left promptly to take care of my family.

Saint Cyprien was small but a very popular seaside tourist city. Every hotel or motel had a sign that said NO VACANCY. My mother had never been in such a situation, she lived a comfortable life. She was near to having a nervous breakdown, upset to see me walking calmly.

It was getting late. We walked all over town with no success at finding even one room. My mother was a Godly woman.

I told her; "Either Jesus is Lord over every area of your life or He is not. "Mother, do you trust God only when things are well? Calm yourself, God never fails, you will see God is going to provide a nice place for us to rest tonight."

Just as I finished saying that, I turned around and saw a lady putting out a sign "Furnished studio for rent by the day." And we just walked right in.

After a couple days, resting and praying together.

My mother wanted to take all of us back home with her; I believed I was called to stay in Perpignan.

My mother took Esther and Eric back home to reconnect with the family.

Perpignan was also overcrowded with tourists. I was walking down a narrow street with Nouchka in her little folding carriage, praying silently.

An old lady was standing on her doorstep and said; "What a beautiful baby you have here, are you a tourist?"

I answered; "No, but do you have a room to rent?"

She said; "I live in a small apartment, but just across the street go to that office, they will help you to find something."

I entered the office. There were a lot of people sitting there waiting for their turn. I heard people talking to the lady behind the desk, asking for jobs.

Finally, I was called. The lady clerk asked what kind of job I was looking for. I told her any kind. She asked me to give her my references. I told her I did not have any. I told her about my last job as a waitress and went on to tell her what I did previously with public relations for Christian mission as an interpreter for English, Spanish, Italian and German. She asked me my phone number and my address. I told her I don't have any. She seemed surprised. She looked at Nouchka and me, then stood up and went in the back room to call someone.

She came back and said; "Monsieur Faran, the president of the chamber of commerce, will give you an audience."

A gentleman accompanied us upstairs. In a ceremonial gesture, he introduced me to the luxurious office of the president who was sitting behind his desk looking very important.

(I learned later that he was the most important man in that town and elections had a lot to do with him.)

He stood up and made a gesture for me to sit in a red velvet armchair near his desk.

Monsieur Faran "What is your problem ? Why are you in the street in Perpignan with a young child."

I looked at him and with respect, I told him; "Monsieur Faran, I have a small problem, because I am not important, but I observed that you are a very important man, and you must have big problems. I believe God sent me here today for you, to tell you that He loves you and that there is nothing impossible with God, I am a living proof of it."

I witnessed to him with passion and was possessed by the Holy Spirit. I don't remember what I said but it was about his work and his position in the government.

Monsieur Faran was a Catholic. He asked me a lot of questions about my faith and my life. Nouchka was quiet and smiling.

Monsieur Faran said to go back to his secretary as she will take care of us.

The secretary told me she was able to have a room in the local hotel and to stay there until she contacts me. Everything is paid and she told me to go to the "Secours Catholic." English meaning of "emergency aid" is in the same street to pick up diapers, food, whatever else I needed.

YES! GOD did it again, when you put others before your own needs.

A couple of days later, an amazing surprise was waiting for me coming back from witnessing. I had gotten a job at the Palais des Rois De Majorque XII – XIV (Palace of the Kings of Majorca), to be the hostess translator. There was a waiting list of one year for this position.

Monsieur Faran thought that I was more competent with my historic and art experience and fluency in five languages.

Like many Catholics, Monsieur Faran used "The Secour Catholic" agency to give out financial help.

The director lady of the agency, confessed to me that Monsieur Faran always did charity in secret and she quoted;

MATTHEW 6:3-4," BUT WHEN YOU DO A CHARITABLE DEED, DO NOT LET YOUR LEFT HAND KNOW WHAT YOUR RIGHT HAND IS DOING, THAT YOUR CHARITABLE DEED MAY BE IN SECRET, AND

YOUR FATHER WHO SEES IN SECRET WILL HIMSELF REWARD YOU OPENLY."

She said Monsieur Faran told them to tell me to look for an apartment and they will pay for it until I am able to take charge of my own expenses.

My first day at "Le Palais", I discovered it was a very busy place with architects, a conservator of the art, archaeologist, a person to restore art, gardeners, guides and doorkeepers. A very joyous company welcomed me with curiosity. All those men found out very fast that I did not want them to go to hell.

Every morning, we all came early to have breakfast together and prepare for the day. Little Nouchka was with a babysitter during the hours I was working, finishing at 4 pm.

In the south of France, it was always a challenge to find an apartment to rent. Everybody working in the Palais with all their contacts tried to find a house for me and my children, but there was nothing available.

Monsieur Lliado, the professor in charge of restoring art, was talking with me and said; "The end of the touristic season is near. I am sure that my friend who has a vacant villa will be able to help out."

He called; the smile on his face gave way to a disappointed expression.

He said; "My friend has an army of people working there to remodel the villa...What are you going to do?"

I answered him; "If God wants me to stay in Perpignan, He will open a door for me. If not, I will know it is not His will for me to be here."

Monsieur Lliado "But Elisabeth you must be realistic and have your feet on the ground. I believe in God, but you cannot expect God to answer all our needs. He has more important things to do in this whole world than look for an apartment."

My answer to him was; "I serve a mighty God. He loves me so much that He died for me. My God cares. You will see. God will bring me the key of a three-bedroom apartment near a school and on the first floor right here."

(First floor was important since I still had stomach pain since Nouchka was born, and doing stairs was not easy.)
Our conversation got interrupted by the guide, who needed me to interpret. Walking together to the main entrance, the guide was furious, telling me what had just happened to him;

"Can you imagine, people have no respect. My tenant of four years just came and gave me the key of the apartment I rented to him, with no warning."

I asked him; "Is it an F3, first floor, near a school?"

He answered "Yes in the best neighborhood of Perpignan near the Mayor's house, do you know those people?"

I told him; "No, but I know one thing, that it is my apartment that I just claimed it from God. Please give me the keys."

I walked very fast with the wind in my step, praising God, to Monsieur Lliado's office chanting Halleluiah! Halleluiah! With the Keys in my hand, Monsieur Lliado listened with his mouth opened in amazement. God became more accessible to him that very day.

The rest of the time I worked there, he honored me with great respect, inviting me to his home to meet his family. He furnished my new apartment with some of the furniture from the historic monastery that he owned, which overflowed with antique furniture. He made sure everything was there for the arrival of the children, with my brother Daniel. With his wife Odette, who was an excellent cook.

LOISIRS

M. Daniel Durst, nouveau président des pêcheurs à la mouche

Il succède à M. André Bencetti qui avait souhaité passer la main.

Lors de l'assemblée générale, le Club Comtois des Pêcheurs à la Mouche de Montbéliard a élu un nouveau président, M. Daniel Durst qui succède à M. André Bencetti lequel avait souhaité mettre fin à ses fonctions. Le nouveau responsable a fait l'éloge de son prédécesseur pour ses cinq années passées à la tête de l'association.

On a exposé les projets du club : deux voyages en Bohê-me-Moravie (république Tchèque) du 12 au 16 mai et du 2 au 6 octobre 1994 pour des sommes assez modestes (1.500 F environ.)

Les sorties régionales seront plus fréquentes les dimanches en rivière de 2è catégorie, pêche carnassier en streamer ou pêche en étangs et réservoirs, truites arc-en-ciel, farios, saumons de Fontaine etc...

Pour la continuité, deux jeudis soirs par mois sont pré-vus pour le montage, soirées débats, vidéos... Prochaine rencontre le jeudi 2 décembre, salle du centre médico-social de la Chiffogne à 20 heures. On peut téléphoner pour tous renseignements à M. Daniel Durst au 81-91-16-28 entre 8 h et 12 h ou de 13 h à 19 heures.

Une étude sera réalisée pour un projet de pêche en réservoir sur la zone de loi-sirs, le long de l'autoroute. Il faut en moyenne entre 4 et 5 hectares. Les réservoirs se développent en France, a fait remarquer le président, ce qui permet aux pêcheurs de ne pas interrompre leur acti-vité pendant la fermeture des rivières 1ère catégorie.

Le nouveau bureau : 1er vice-président : M. André Ben-cetti, 2ème vice-président : M. Daniel Ory, trésorier : M. Fré-déric Delage, secrétaire : M. Jacques Panchot.

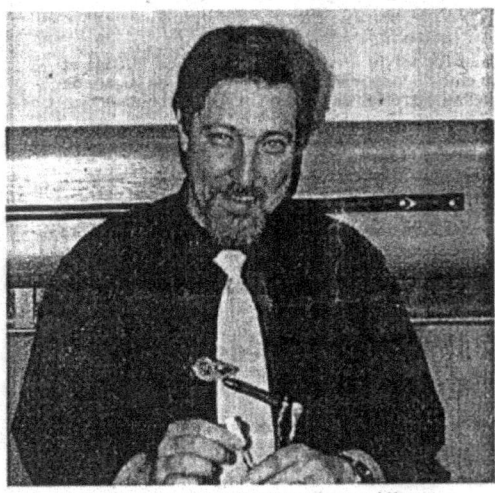

M. Daniel Durst a rendu hommage à son prédécesseur.

Chapter 18

A CUP OF MILK

Michelle Bousquet visited me, she became my social worker. She was filling out papers for us in order to have assistance; I asked her why I would receive so much.

Michelle said; "Why not you? All the Arab immigrants get it. The social services in France will pay you sufficiently to be able to take care of your three children plus pay your rent, utility bills, provide a dishwasher and a laundry machine and a helper for the home for four hours a day and all your medical needs."

Michelle was worried about me as my health was deteriorating. She sent her doctor to my home hoping he could provide a cure or at least something to help me cope with my illness.

I did not understand why God had not healed me from all those malignant tumors. I continued to visit and pray for the sick in the local hospital, and many were healed, yet I was not.

Esther 9 years old, on her days off from school would go with me to the hospital to visit the sick. Esther saw me pray and hug older ladies with sores on their faces and bodies. I told her she did not have to do that.

But Esther said; "I want to do what you are doing!"

Madame Marasse, who loved Esther, carried an emergency kit with alcohol pads in her purse to make sure to clean Esther after visiting the sick.

When I was too weak to go out, witnessing. I prayed; "Lord I am too tired to go out, please send them into our home for me to witness."

God answered my request. I hardly ever locked my door and one late night someone woke me up. I opened my eyes and saw three anxious faces asking if I was Elisabeth. Someone from Montpellier had given them my address. They asked if they could sleep on the floor in the living room. It was winter and they were cold and hungry having walked for miles trying to find jobs and a place to stay. I welcomed them. The two boys slept on the sofa in the living room, and the girl slept with me in the double bed to share the blankets.

One day the doorbell rang, Esther opened the door, to our surprise; it was Italian Jacomo from THE BABES RANCH in Certaldo in Italy. He introduced his wife, Mary.

Four years ago, Jacomo had been in a seminary studying to become a Catholic priest. He was curious about the Revolution for Jesus and had come to investigate us. He did argue with our beliefs, especially about the rapture. I answered him only with Bible verses of what Jesus said, telling him the rapture would not happen until the Gospel has been preached to the whole world. We are not there yet, which is why we need a lot of believers to go out and evangelize.

Jacomo would retort; "What do you know about it? Only God knows! Show me where it is in the Bible!"

In Matthew 24:8-31 Jesus said; "ALL THESE ARE THE BEGINNING OF SORROWS AND THIS GOSPEL OF THE KINGDOM WILL BE PREACHED IN ALL THE WORLD AS A WITNESS TO ALL THE NATIONS AND THEN THE END WILL COME. AND UNLESS THOSE DAYS WERE SHORTENED NO FLESH WOULD BE SAVED BUT FOR THE ELECT'S

SAKE THOSE DAYS WILL BE SHORTENED. IMMEDIATELY AFTER THE TRIBULATION OF THOSE DAYS, THE SUN WILL BE DARKENED AND THE MOON WILL NOT GIVE ITS LIGHT, THE STARS WILL FALL FROM HEAVEN AND THE POWERS OF THE HEAVENS WILL BE SHAKEN...

Jacomo interrupted me and said; "That does not talk about the rapture!"

I told him; "Please let me continue"

THEN THE SIGN OF THE SON OF MAN WILL APPEAR IN HEAVEN AND THEN ALL THE TRIBES OF THE EARTH WILL MOURN AND THEY WILL SEE THE SON OF MAN COMING ON THE CLOUDS OF HEAVEN WITH POWER AND GREAT GLORY AND HE WILL SEND HIS ANGELS WITH THE GREAT SOUND OF A TRUMPET AND THEY WILL GATHER TOGETHER HIS ELECT FROM THE FOUR WINDS FROM ONE END OF HEAVEN TO THE OTHER.

After that, he did meditate on what Jesus said and stayed with us at the VOLPE.

To see Jacomo in front of me after such a long time!

I exclaimed; "What a surprise! Please tell me what happened to you?"

Jacomo, emotionally, answered; "I was looking for you because after you left, I got baptized in the Holy Spirit and the Lord kept reminding me to go on the mission field just like you. Do you remember in the "Volpe" it was winter and I got very sick. You and your children prayed for me. Everybody else went to do their daily chores. Milk was precious, reserved only for the nursery and the young children. Esther and Eric had only one cup of milk a day. You brought me one cup of hot milk. For me, to see the love you had, changed my heart. I wanted to find you to thank you, Esther and Eric, from the bottom of my heart."

I remembered that very day. Yes! It was cold in that big house. The huge fire place warmed up only the first floor. While preparing breakfast for Esther and Eric we felt sorry for Jacomo.

Esther Said; "This hot milk is so good. We must give some to poor Jacomo that will make him feel better."

I told her, but we have only one cup for you and one cup for Eric.

Esther said; "I can share"

Eric said; "Me too"

We filled up a third cup and I brought the precious gift to Jacomo.

Jacomo said "But that is the children's milk, I cannot accept it"

I told him it was Esther's and Eric's desire, hoping that the milk will heal him because there was love in that milk.
I never forgot the look in his eyes as he held that precious milk and drank it very slowly, tears running down his face.

BECAUSE OF A CUP OF MILK JACOMO BECAME A MISSIONARY ON HIS WAY TO INDIA!

What looks like nothing to someone, to someone else a cup of milk can be very precious.

PSALM 133:1, BEHOLD HOW GOOD AND HOW PLEASANT IT IS FOR BRETHREN TO DWELL TOGETHER IN UNITY!

November was often a sad month. More people were in need and with no shelter. An American couple from the Revolution with two small children and another one on the way rang the door-bell. The woman who was expecting looked exhausted. The whole crew was very thin and in great need of everything. I understood their situation because I had walked in the same road. They spoke only a few words in French using a dictionary to communicate.

A French sister in the Lord, in Montpellier, who had looked after Esther and Eric, had given them my new address.

I told them to have a bath and relax, while I washed their clothing. I gave them clothes to change into and I prepared dinner.

The market did not have any vegetables or fruit to give away that day. No longer was I too proud to ask for food from the grocers that would be thrown out by end of day so I could feed my full house.

But today we had only a half pound of rice, which I put garlic parsley and small pieces of tomatoes.

Rebecca came in the kitchen to help, she exclaimed; "Oh Elisabeth that is just enough for the children."

I told her; "Don't worry God loves us, it is written that He always supplies for our needs."

Together we started to sing! "MY GOD SHALL SUPPLY ALL MY NEEDS ACCORDING TO HIS RICHES IN GLORY."

A ring from the door interrupted our joyous worship. There was a man standing at the door with a huge box.

He said; "Can I come in. This is heavy!"

He explained that he was having his lunch, at the Giral restaurant in Montpellier, telling them that he was on his way to Perpignan to visit his mother. Then the Giral's got excited and asked him to bring this box for me, in exchange of a free lunch.

I opened the box with everybody standing around to see what was in it. The box was full of all kinds of delicious food, steaks, pasta, smoked meat, salami, ham and much more. It was enough to last at least one week.

Everybody gave Glory to God!

The man who brought the box was so surprised when I told him he was an angel sent by God, to answer our prayers.

He blushed and said; "I am not an angel I did not go to church since I was a Boy!"

I explained to him, God used Him, just like He did with the prophet Balaam, using his donkey to speak to him to save his master's life.

God can use anyone and anything to answer the prayer of His children.

He concluded with laughter that he was the angel donkey.

Esther was only eight years old when she wrote her first song, "BABIES, THEY ARE SO SWEET" For her little baby sister Nouchka. Esther was like a little Cinderella, except unlike Cinderella, she was very much loved by her family.

The missionaries that came and stayed for a while always took Esther with them to witness. Esther would interpret and sing playing her guitar.

Most of the time the adult evangelists would be rejected, but when Esther started singing it was magic......Everyone would listen, Esther had a unique voice for a little girl, with a vibrant deep tone. This was God's gift to her.

She would sing in French; "ALL THE CHILDREN NEED A LOT OF LOVE, LIKE A LITTLE CHILD LORD I NEED YOU, WHEN I AM ALONE YOU COME TO RESCUE ME, YOU ARE THE ONLY ONE THAT MAKES MY VOICE SING. I FORGET MY PAST I NEVER REGRETTED IT...YOU ARE MY LIFE JESUS, I LOVE YOU, YOU ARE MY LIFE JESUS, I NEED YOU, IF TODAY I AM NOT THE SAME IT IS BECAUSE OF YOU, YOU ARE MY LIFE JESUS, I NEED YOU, YOU ARE MY LIFE JESUS, I LOVE YOU."

After the song, people were ready to listen to the evangelist.

Every day I asked God for strength. I was so thankful to be loved by God, and to be able to be alive for my three children.

It is impossible to compare the love of God with human love. That is the most important thing someone can ever experience. It is so easy to be an agnostic when you never ever have a relationship with Jesus.

Two wonderful missionaries stayed more than a month with us, until they found something to rent. Mark was Canadian and his wife Anna was American. They found a small apartment to rent in Narbonne, a city near Perpignan.

In Narbonne the radio was announcing a big contest for singers of every age. The first prize was a recording studio offering to make a record.

Anna and Mark signed up Esther, who was at this time12 years old. I was not able to attend because of my health, but the radio broadcasted this program to all the radio stations in France.

Most of the contestants were professionals with only a few amateurs. The crowd was wild making fun of the contestants; some troublemakers threw tomatoes at some of them.

Esther was next, trembling in nervousness.

Esther said; "Anna... I cannot do this I am going to faint!"

Mark and Anna put their hands on Esther, praying in tongues.

Esther felt peace and said; "OK, I am going to do it."

As she walked on the stairs to the stage, she tripped over an electric cord. Everybody in the audience laughed.

The spokesperson asked her age, then asked her what she was going to sing and told her to give her music to the band.

Esther answered him; "I am 12 years old, I am going to sing "LES ENFANTS (The children) I don't need a band. My guitar is all I need."

The speaker was amused, the crowd was laughing and Esther was trembling.

Esther closed her eyes. Then she started to play and sing. The whole crowd became silent.

Esther sang her favorite song; "ALL THE CHILDREN NEED A LOT OF LOVE LIKES A LITTLE CHILD LORD I NEED YOU..."

Mark and Anna told me some people were wiping their face from tears. When Esther finished and opened her eyes, to her surprise there was an ovation. She won the hearts of many and opened the door for Mark and Anna to witness to the people.

After a big debate by the selection committee, Esther received the 2nd place. This was only because she was so young and would have more opportunities than the group that won 1st place. They needed that prize more than Esther, but she was happy because the only reason for her to be there was to be a witness for God.

Chapter 19

POLICE HUNTING A MURDERER

Driving to the next town, a young man was sitting against a tree with his backpack next to him, he looked very miserable, he was not hitchhiking.

I prayed; "Lord if you want me to pick him up, he will be right there on my way back home."

Two hours later, I found the guy in the same spot. I told him to get in my car. He had a hard time trying to stand on his feet. He had a broken ankle he got up and finally got in the car. I asked him what happened to him, his answer was; "NOT SPEAK FRENCH". I tried English, German, Italian and Spanish, his answer was always; "NO" He needed medical help. On the road to the hospital, I was stopped by a bunch of police. They looked with suspicion at my passenger. They asked me to get out of the car.

One policeman said; "Do not pick up any strangers on the road, a hitchhiker has murdered two women yesterday in that region but the third woman in the car has survived, the whole country is on alert to find him. It is obvious that you don't listen to the news."

I started to witness to them; "Jesus died on the cross for the sinners, even a murderer must have a chance to repent. If I get killed doing my job, I will go right to heaven, your job is more dangerous, and if you get killed do you know if you go to heaven or hell?"

I gave them a pamphlet with the prayer of salvation in it.

After the hospital took care of the stranger's foot, I took him home to feed him, cleaned him up and gave him clothes to change. I always had extra clothing in every size from donations.

Danny was his name. He was scratching his body and little Nouchka tried to help him by putting powder on his back, but nothing helped. I noticed that his body was covered with infected sores. I took him to the doctor that was on the same street.

The doctor told me it was a very contagious disease. I had to burn all his clothing and everything his skin had been in contact with. I told him my children had hugged him.

The doctor said we should all go to be tested immediately at the hospital and for Danny to stay there in quarantine.

The children were in school. After I left Danny in the hospital the first thing back home, I went on my knees and asked God to protect my children because we did all with a merciful heart. I knew it was an attack from the enemy. I opened my Bible in the middle and Psalm 91 jumped out in my face.

"HE WHO DWELLS IN THE SECRET PLACE OF THE MOST HIGH SHALL ABIDE UNDER THE SHADOW OF THE ALMIGHTY I WILL SAY OF THE LORD HE IS MY REFUGE AND MY FORTRESS MY GOD IN HIM I WILL TRUST SURELY, HE SHALL DELIVER YOU FROM THE SNARE OF THE FOWLER AND FROM THE PERILOUS PESTILENCE HE SHALL COVER YOU WITH HIS FEATHER AND UNDER HIS WINGS YOU SHALL TAKE REFUGE HIS TRUTH SHALL BE YOUR SHIELD AND BUCKLER YOU SHALL NOT BE AFRAID OF THE TERROR BY NIGHT NOR OF THE ARROW THAT FLIES BY DAY NOR THE PESTILENCE THAT WALKS IN

DARKNESS."

All my fears vanished and everything worked out exactly the way God said it would.

After the quarantine, I picked up Danny. He was speaking in broken French much better now. He said he was from Holland, one language I did not speak, so I ordered a Bible in his language to make sure he could participate in our daily Bible study. He was weak, skinny and in poor health.

I told him he should go back to his family, who must be worried about him. He confessed that he was an orphan and had no one to go back to.

I told him that God loved him, that He is the father of the orphans.

He responded with rage; "If God loves me, why did he not let my mother abort me, I wish I was never born! I hate Esther, Eric and Nouchka. Why do they have a mother and not me? I did not hurt anyone... I hate you all!"

He left, came back the next day and apologized. I gave him a hug and told him if it was OK with him, we would be his family.

I explained to my children that Danny was sad because he never had a father and a mother, but that God gave you a mother and we must try to help him to know he will never be alone anymore if he will just accept Jesus in his heart.

Nouchka was three years old and she would sing to him in French; "Shizue! (the way she pronounced JESUS) is my best friend, he is always with me, I can depend on Him, and his love is free... Ooooooooh! YES!"

A few weeks later, Danny pretended to read the Bible and when we prayed, he would politely put his head down but never participate.

I told him; "It was not God who made you an orphan, it was Satan the prince of this world who delighted in seeing people suffers, he is the father of all the evil that covers this earth. God created only good things for Adam and Eve so they could live in perfect joy and peace forever. In Genesis 2:16 it is written; "EVERY TREE OF THE GARDEN YOU MAY FREELY EAT BUT OF THE TREE OF KNOWLEDGE OF GOOD AND EVIL YOU SHALL NOT EAT FOR IN THE DAY THAT YOU EAT OF IT YOU SHALL SURELY DIE."

Satan tested them, they followed Satan's advice and they disobeyed. God was so grieved because God is Holy, sin cannot stay in his presence. Adam and Eve went to live with Satan on earth and they died. We are all descendants of Adam and Eve or from the fallen angels. We are all born with an evil nature. The only way to be reconnected with God is to be purified by the blood of Jesus Christ, the son of God, who became the divine sacrifice for whoever believes in Him will never die but have eternal life. If we ask Jesus to come in our hearts, we became free from a tormented evil spirit, if we read his words; we will grow strong in the Holy Spirit. That is to be born again.

If you hate yourself now, you will surely like the new you. This does not mean everything will go right, but when trouble comes, you will never feel alone, the power of the Spirit of Jesus Christ will give you strength and peace that surpasses all human understanding."

Danny said; "Yes, I would like to be a new person, but I need to confess something to you first. I fear that you are going to be very upset and want me to go away."

I thought, Oh Lord, what kind of sin did he commit?
I told him; "I will not judge you, just say it."

Danny started speaking in perfect French with no accent. He said; "I was lying, I am French from Normandy. I was in the orphanage until I was 18."

I started laughing so hard, remembering all the trouble Danny went through pretending to be from Holland, even writing letters in this language to show me and asking for an envelope to send to his friend Herve... and now finding out it was actually a recipe in several languages that he had found on a glue box.

Many years later Danny went to China as a missionary where he married a Chinese girl.

The apartment was sold; the owner gave me one month's notice to find another place to live, after living in that nice place for five years. I had three more young guys. Danny has two friends Herve and Didier who had come from the same national orphanage. Herve was very difficult for me; he had no respect for God, making stupid jokes about my big sign in wood carving that was on the top of the wall, which said: THE LORD IS MY SHEPHERD I SHALL NOT WANT.

I told everyone I was not the one who provided their shelter, food and clothes. It was God.

Herve lifted his glass and said; "I drink to the bloody stupid one who paid for it!"

I stood up, told Herve to pick up his bag and to go and never come back.

He was surprised and said; "That was a joke!"

I opened the door without saying a word. Danny and Didier started interceding for him.

Herve said; "I cannot believe in God, even if he does exist why I should? He does not care about me. I was four years old and my three brothers were six, eight and ten. One day, when we came back home from school, we did not find our mother in the kitchen. My older brother and I had the chore to go down to the cellar and pick out some potatoes for dinner. Under the pile of potatoes, a hand appeared. It was my mother's hand. My alcoholic father had killed her and had hidden her under the potatoes before he took off. It did not take long for the police to catch him. All four of us were separated and put in orphanages. I never saw my brothers again. My mother was dead, my father was in jail for life, and you are telling me about a God who loves me?" Herve started to laugh hysterically....

I could not find anything to say. I was heartbroken for the boy. I thought this could be my own children's story.

After this, I became more patient and prayed specifically for Herve. Many months later, he received the baptism of the Holy Spirit.

The next town was only about 10 miles away from Perpignan, where there were a lot of vineyards. The land was the property of the D'ORIOLA family; their Castle was famous for their wines. I went to ring the doorbell. Christopher D'Oriola opened the door, he was on his way out but very nicely, he took the time to invite me in and listen to what I had to say. He told me to bring the guys the next morning at 7 am so that they could start working for LES VENDANGES (the "Grape Harvest").

The next morning Monsieur D'Oriola introduced me to his wife Paula. While having breakfast together, they were very curious to know my story. I told them about the love of Jesus Christ and the power in His blood.

They told me about the loss of their son that had happened just a few months prior, in a motorcycle accident. We became close friends.

One morning their Catholic priest was there. He was waiting to meet me and he looked very suspicious.

He asked me; "Who gave you the authority to do what you are doing?

"I answered him, Jesus said; "FOR I WAS HUNGRY AND YOU GAVE ME FOOD. I WAS THIRSTY AND YOU GAVE ME DRINK. I WAS A STRANGER AND YOU TOOK ME IN. I WAS NAKED AND YOU CLOTHED ME. I WAS SICK AND YOU VISITED ME. I WAS IN PRISON AND YOU CAME TO ME. I SAY TO YOU AS YOU DID IT TO THE LEAST OF THESE YOU DID IT TO ME." (Matthew25:35-40)

I just obey the Lord, like most people do.

The priest stood up, excused himself and left with a sour face.

Paula was laughing; "That is the first time that I have seen him speechless, like you said, the Word of God never fails."

I was wondering where little Nouchka was. There was perfect silence in the house. I opened my bedroom door and there she was in ecstasy, looking at the wall radiantly, with tears of joy on her face. I felt the Spirit of the Lord in the room, in silence I just watched her until Nouchka spoke these words;

"I want to go to Jesus, I want to stay with Him. Please maman let me go with Jesus."

I hugged my little girl. I did not know what all this meant. I thought maybe the Lord is going to take Nouchka.

"O LORD OUR LORD HOW EXCELLENT IS YOUR NAME IN ALL THE EARTH. YOU WHO SET YOUR GLORY ABOVE THE HEAVEN! OUT OF THE MOUTH OF BABES YOU HAVE ORDAINED STRENGTH." (Psalm 8:1-2)

Chapter 20

MAROCCO

Christopher and Paula offered us the use of one of their properties, the "Mas Maroc". Christopher's plan was to remodel the farm in the next year for his daughter, but until then we could use it for free, along with all my entourage who were growing in numbers. The guys installed electricity and water inside the home, painted the first floor, and wallpapered the bedrooms on the second floor.

I brought them to church every Sunday. One of the young pastors of the "Assembly of God" church became enthusiastic when I told him five of those guys were ready to be baptized.

The next week a delegation of two pastors and two elders arrived at Mas Maroc. (Called The Refuge). They asked to speak to me in private. The Senior pastor told me he would not baptize a bunch of hippies in his church. He had a meeting with the board of members and they considered their church to be too respectable to have an invasion of hippies coming in. That was 1978.

I answered; "I guess Jesus would not be welcomed in your church because he had long hair and hung out with sinners, and I don't think his disciples were so clean, living on the road and sleeping in parks."

They left, except the young pastor.

He said; "I will baptize them here. Jesus' disciples always baptized in rivers and that is what we will do."

The guys were not surprised at being rejected by the self-righteous old men of the church.

They said; "We must leave those Pharisees alone and live like Jesus, he also was rejected by the priests."

I told them; "We are the living stone, obeying the Lord, witnessing. We are the body of Christ. We are the church!"

The farm was producing a lot of lettuce. Christopher told me I could do whatever I wanted with all that was growing on the farm. I contacted the manager of the university cafeteria and got his OK to sell them 200 lettuces every week for the cafeteria. Fruit trees, olive trees and potatoes grew in abundance, which kept everybody busy and praising God.

During summer vacation, Esther and Eric went to a Christian camp. Most of the residents had gotten summer jobs in different locations. I left a young couple Brigitte and Hughes in charge of "The Refuge". The name of the farm was "MAS MAROC", translated into English is "MOROCCO FARM." Danny said that the Lord told him in a dream that we must go to Morocco in North Africa.

I answered him; "Do you know they kill Christians and Jews in Morocco? Hmm! But to be sure it is really God we are going to hitchhike."

Danny was reluctant, believing that we must take the car so Nouchka, who was six years old at the time, could sleep in the car instead of walking on the road.

I said; "I want to be sure that it's God's will to go there. If it is, He will provide us with the ride, so we will know for sure it was God's idea and not yours."

We left home with a light backpack, walking on a road in the direction towards Spain, witnessing to everyone we came in contact with. At one place we stopped to start to hitchhike.

After less than five minutes, a car stopped and carried us for about 200 miles all the way to the border of Spain. We had to traverse the entire length of Spain to get to Morocco.

Nouchka was a happy traveler, always finding a way to play on the side of the road while waiting for a car to pick us up. One couple stopped and drove us up all the way to Malaga, the south of Spain, near the border of Morocco. The couple had a beautiful home near the sea, and they hosted us in their home where they were entertaining a group of people of different nationalities. I was able to witness to all of them.

Back on the road, I prayed; "Lord, if you want us to go to Morocco for a specific reason that only You know, please provide an angel going towards our destination."

Very soon a huge dark-skinned Moroccan guy stopped, driving a big car, and he

Said; "Guys, get in my car, it's too late for you to be on the road."

I exclaimed; "You are the angel I just asked God to send us!"

Akim was his name. After listening about Danny's dream, he told us that he was fasting and praying for a messenger who would go for him to visit his family in Fes. Fes was far in the middle of Morocco.

He said; "The government is so corrupt it is dangerous for me to go there. My oldest son applied for a passport and paid a lot of money to people who promised to help, but it's been years and nothing has worked out for him. Please can you bring a letter with money for my family? They are in great need."

I prayed, Lord whatever you want us to do, we are willing. As Fes was the direction that God wanted us to go.

God was teaching us that His eyes are on everyone who seeks Him. Akim gave us hospitality. At sundown, he unrolled a little carpet, covered his head, kneeled down and bowed, reciting his prayers. To show respect for our host, we prayed silently. It was Ramadan.

The next day Akim told us he believed Jesus was coming back and drove us out to the main road going to Morocco.

Soon an RV driven by a Jehovah's Witness couple stopped. They were going to Fes! INCREDIBLE! GOD blew my mind! For a CHRISTIAN born again, not blinded by religion, you can SEE that God does not care about religion. But He looks to the heart.

That is why Jesus told the story about the GOOD SAMARITAN.

It was a long and dangerous trip, but God provided this couple, who went to Fes every year to do business. They knew the road and the customs.

Arriving in Fes, we found Akim's family and gave them the envelope with the precious content. Akim's family's hospitality was fantastic. Christian hospitality is very pale in comparison.

I started to understand why God had sent us to that country; it was to learn why so few of them would embrace Christianity.

Like this Christian business man who was a representative for a company in Dubai, said; in the middle of a meeting, all the Muslims left the room the moment they heard the call to prayer from the mosque. They did not want to miss the time of prayer at any cost.

He heard the Lord clearly telling him;

"HOW ARE YOU GOING TO TELL THESE PEOPLE WHO PRAY FIVE TIMES A DAY ABOUT JESUS, IF YOU DON'T HAVE A PRAYER LIFE YOURSELF?"

Our ways are so self-centered and their ways are so humble. They give the best they have to a foreigner, like their own bed and the only piece of meat in the couscous was a goat's foot and they insisted on giving it to us.

It was Ramadan, 40 days no drinking, no food, from sunrise until sunset. It was summer. The heat was over 100 degrees and most people would do hard work during the day while fasting and no water. People were dying every day from dehydration. To show them respect, I observed their fasting with the exception that I would drink some water.

Nouchka played with a bunch of little girls around the house, she observed those little girls her age working like adults, scrubbing floors, making bread, taking care of baby sisters or brothers. Many children lost their mothers, some died after so many births. Even though, they played, laughed, danced and sang with Nouchka.

I sat every day on the floor with a lot of curious women from the neighborhood, witnessing, answering questions with scriptures without using my Bible.

At the end of a conversation, one lady said; "We never heard anybody speak with so much wisdom."

I responded; "That is not my word but God's Word. Jesus the Christ, revealing to us the heart of God and the healing power in the blood of his son Jesus."

Jared, the devoted older son, was the father figure of the family. He explained to me about Muslim beliefs. They believed the Bible was taken into heaven with Jesus when people wanted to kill him. That it is why Jesus did not die on the cross and did not pay the high price for our salvation. Muslims believe that the Bible was falsified by the Jews.

I witnessed about my dreams and visions from the Lord and the power of the healing blood of Jesus Christ.

Soon after speaking about Jesus' healing, Nouchka got very sick with a high temperature, from their infected water.

I prayed but Nouchka's fever was worse the next day.

Danny got really mad at the devil. He grabbed Nouchka shook her and screamed;

"You evil spirits of sickness get out of Nouchka now in the name of JESUS! JESUS! JESUS!"

Nouchka stood up and started to dance. Danny was on his knees, his whole body shaking under the power of the Holy Spirit.

Sometime after this, the youngest boy of the house was limping. His leg had turned dark blue and was much more swollen than his other leg. He had a bad cut under his foot from walking without shoes and his leg got infected. His mother, Akim's wife, took him to a clinic. He had a fever and they wanted to open up his foot to drain the pus out. The boy begged them to wait until tomorrow. The doctor insisted that by tomorrow the infection might be so bad that they may have to cut off his leg.

The boy took off running home looking for Danny and me to pray for him.

I did and that same evening his leg was healed. Glory to God! This was the result of that little boy's faith.

Jared the older brother, a university student, was the one who had been asking the government for a passport for years. He was so depressed to be a prisoner of his own country that he tried to take his life.

I told him I will go with him and talk to the governor.

Jared smile; "That is not France; this is Morocco it is impossible to go near the governor if you are not an official delegated by your country."

I told him; "With God ALL things are possible."

Jared said; "Let's go"

It was a long walk from the Medina (old town) to the new town to arrive at the palace where the governor's office was. It also head-quartered his military force. When we arrived at the palace, the guards at the entrance stopped us.

I told them; "Tell the Governor that Michele Hinman wants to see him!"

They left and came back with two high ranking military officials. They looked at me and my passport, and then they talked together in Arabic. Then the soldiers told me to follow them and for Jared and Danny to wait downstairs in the lobby. One officer introduced me to the governor.

The governor looked at me with a haughty expression.

He asked; "Do I know you?"

I said; "I am visiting, and I am here to ask you the favor of releasing the passport of one of the family members of my dearest friends. He applied years ago, paid lot of money and never got his passport."

The governor rudely interrupted me;

"It is not your business to claim a passport for one of our citizens."

I answered him; "Oh yes, it is my business. This dear family welcomed me with such incredible hospitality that only the people of your country are able to do. I love Morocco and I love your people. I invited Jared to come to visit us, but he told me he cannot get his passport and explained why. That is why I am here today."

The governor said; "Why should I get involved with this? I don't take care of passports; I have much more important things to do."

I said; "Sir, it is Ramadan "SIYAM" a symbol of faith; you notice that I am a Christian wearing my little cross, but I observe Ramadan because of my respect for your religion. You observe Ramadan too. I am sure that Allah will be pleased if you do an act of charity that only you can do. You are a descendant of Abraham, through Ismael, I am a descendant of Abraham through Jeshua ha Mashiah (Jesus the Christ), our father Abraham worshiped the God who created all things.

God said He does not take pleasure in sacrifices, but He takes pleasure in love and in a merciful heart."

The governor stood up from his desk, walked to his window and paused for one minute. Then he called one of his officials to prepare a release form in Arabic.

He signed and said; "Madame Hinman your request is accepted", giving me the paper.

Jared could not believe his eyes and his ears. He could not stop laughing and suddenly he was feeling very light. He just learned that to have Jesus is to have direct access to God and God answers prayer in the name above all names "JESUS THE CHRIST."

Mission accomplished. It was time to hit the road to go back home to pick up Esther and Eric, their summer camp vacation would be over in a week. We traveled back safely and by the grace of God we arrived in time.

PSALM 5:11 BUT LET ALL THOSE REJOICE WHO PUT THEIR TRUST IN YOU. LET THEM EVER SHOUT FOR JOY BECAUSE YOU DEFEND THEM LET THOSE ALSO WHO LOVE YOUR NAME BE JOYFUL IN YOU.

Chapter 21

THE CHATELAINE OF SALIGNAC

After one year, it was time to move again. Two of the guys came back from witnessing with good news that they found a new home up in the mountains of Salignac.

Salignac was a small, old, medieval town, who was well known for cognac and medieval architecture.

The house was big and beautiful with two floors and an attic. When the owner died, a doctor, his widow and children moved to their other property near the sea in the South of France. His widow gave us the keys for us to stay there until they moved back.

On the next street was a small castle. The Chatelaine was also a widow who lived there with her three children. The oldest son, Benoit, was always traveling to Paris back and forth doing concerts. He was a composer of music for films. His younger brother Remi, 19 years old, was not an artist, but he was a dreamer, and lived in his fantasy world. The young people from the little town made fun of him but he ignored them, not affected by anyone's opinion. Marie 17, the sister was going to college and was very conservative, always well dressed. We connected right away and they invited us to their castle for dinner to eat "La Fondue".

The school teachers, along with the town's mayor, made a surprise visit. They said a bunch of schoolgirls talked with Nouchka who was always dancing and making a show. Nouchka told them that her mom taught her ballet. The girls asked their parents, one being the mayor's daughter, to come and ask me to give dance classes in their school.

I told them, I just teach my daughters as a way to help them, to have good posture and a healthy body.

They said; "That is exactly what we want. Some of our girls have scoliosis and need to learn to have good posture. Most of our children dream to become ballerinas. It would be an act of charity if you would extend your teaching to our school, and that will give you an extra income"

I was thinking for a short time watching their anxious faces.

Then I said; "Alright, but I will do it in my home."

The family room was huge and unfurnished. I did not tell them it was because of my poor health. There was plenty of room to put mirrors and bars on the walls. I told them the ballet school could open the following week and would be held on Tuesdays and Fridays after school. They were pleased by such an immediate response.

During Christmas time, the ballet school performed in the town's theater, "The Birth of Jesus."

L'arbre de Noël des écoliers

Samedi après-midi avait lieu à la salle du Foyer la fête de l'arbre de Noël pour nos écoliers. Cette fête traditionnelle, organisée par l'Amicale laïque, a ravi les enfants qui avaient hâte de recevoir les cadeaux.

Les parents étaient là et ont pu applaudir un spectacle enfantin. Les élèves de l'école de danse salignacoise de Mme Hinman ont évolué avec grâce. Pour clôturer un goûter confectionné par les parents a été servi.

It was a success. Esther sang her composition and played her guitar.

Salignac-Eyvigues

Une chanteuse prometteuse

Lorsqu'à l'arbre de Noël de l'Amicale laïque, puis tout dernièrement à la soirée des Rois du troisième âge, le public salignacois eut l'occasion d'applaudir sur scène une adolescente de 14 ans et demi, il pouvait ne pas penser qu'il y avait en cette jeune personne un acquis certain et beaucoup de promesses.

Esther Hinman, c'est l'évidence, a été douée pour le chant. Née d'un père artiste-peintre et écrivain, mort accidentellement dans un accident de montagne, et d'une mère danseuse professionnelle et ancienne chorégraphe au Théâtre de la Télévision à Rome, elle a très tôt manifesté son penchant.

Dès l'âge de 5 ans, elle chantait déjà, s'accompagnant à la guitare. A 7 ans et demi, elle commence à composer et sa première œuvre sera une berceuse pour sa petite sœur.

Par la suite, grandissant, elle va se produire, toujours bénévolement, pour des mouvements charitables, personnes âgées, hôpitaux. Elle est alors remarquée et a pu chanter sur les ondes de Radio Monte-Carlo.

Les pérégrinations de ses parents, exigées par l'activité professionnelle de sa mère, l'ont amenée de Berne à Rome, puis à Montréal, enfin la France et la voilà avec sa mère, son petit frère et sa petite sœur, chez nous, à Salignac.

Des amis ont parlé d'elle à Eddie Warner, le producteur de disques qui, sceptique d'abord en raison de son âge, l'a faite auditionner, puis enregistrer. Il a été enthousiasmé par ce génie encore en herbe. Et alors le producteur a contacté la Télévision française. C'est ainsi que, lorsque les vacances scolaires le lui permettront, la petite Esther, Salignacoise d'aujourd'hui, assistée d'un ensemble musical, va se produire au petit écran.

Tous nos vœux l'accompagnent dans cette voie artistique qu'elle s'est tout naturellement choisie.

Esther Hinman chantait le 10 janvier pour un public du troisième âge. (Ph. René Lacombe).

The next day, the front page of the local newspaper was full of praise for the children's ballet performance, with a picture of Nouchka as an angel of love in the middle of the other ballerinas.

Esther had her picture and a long article about her talent, saying that she was the future "French Joan Baez."

Remi came running over with the newspaper in his hand. He was enthusiastic and he decided to become Esther's agent and to take her to Paris to introduce her to the most famous record producer in France, Eddie Warner, who was a friend of his brother Benoit.

After a long discussion with him and his mother, I finally gave Esther permission to go to Paris during the Christmas vacation.

In Paris, Eddie Warner and his wife gave them hospitality. Eddie Warner was skeptical but because of his regard for Benoit, he agreed to listen to Esther sing. Eddie and his wife were pleasantly surprised, they decided to adopt Esther and make her a star. She would live with them, but because she was only 14 years old, they would need her parent's permission and official papers.

Back home Esther explained to me it was the chance of her life. It was so incredible! That it must be another miracle of God. I asked Esther if she would sing her songs for the Lord.

She said; "Maman, Monsieur Warner said, to start I must sing my song but take out the name of Jesus. In the future when I become successful, I will be able to do what I want, but to start I must do what he says because he knows the business."

I did not like that, but said nothing. I did not want to turn off Esther's hope, she was so excited.

I prayed; "Lord if this opportunity comes from you, I will gladly let Esther go. You are her Father You know what is good for her. If this will pull her away from You, please Lord shut the door. Amen"

One week later, Remi came with a telegram in his hand and said; "I just got this from Paris, (he sat down and put his head in his two hands) I can't believe it, Eddie Warner just died of a heart attack."

God again answered my prayer, in a dramatic way. You don't dare touch his children. I never told anyone about my prayer.

Remi's brother, Benoit, with a group of young producers of television programs, decided to do a promotion tour in every town on the beach. They asked me to participate with Esther, Eric and Nouchka during summer vacation.

Esther produced her first album.

Benoit played his own new music compositions, while Nouchka danced with a white tutu around his synthesizer piano, which was a new thing in the 1980. Eric was helping with the filming crew. I was speaking on local radio stations in every town, promoting the concert and the sale of Esther's record, which we dedicated to benefit the orphans of Cambodia.

When Esther got back to school, she was surprised to find she was a star. Her peers and teachers listened to her songs on the radio and she performed for her school.

PSALM 100:(1) MAKE A JOYFUL SHOUT TO THE LORD ALL "YOU" LANDS! (2), SERVE THE LORD WITH GLADNESS. COME BEFORE HIS PRESENCE WITH SINGING.

Chapter 22

LA COTOREP

One of the guys was in the hospital. He had such brittle bones that whenever he tried to work, he would break something in his body. The doctors said it was not curable because of the severe malnutrition he had suffered since he was born. He was 21 years old in deep depression, with a suicidal mindset. I asked the doctors to give me a medical report to present to the Cotorep, a humanitarian organization that was giving financial help to people with health incapacities.

I called the Cotorep, they sent me papers to fill out. The next month, a secretary called and said that a potential applicant must apply in person for them to have a hearing.

When the hearing was scheduled in a town 65 miles away from Salignac, the guy was still in the hospital and was not able to go.

I decided to go and to represent him. Eric did not have school that day, he wanted to accompany me. We left home very early in the morning.

When we arrived, we found the Cotorep waiting room was already full of people. Every time someone came out from the conference room where the investigation was held, they had a disappointing look in their face.

Eric was concerned, he said; "If we don't bring back a good report to Leduc, do you think he will kill himself? He has already tried two times."

I answered; "There will not be a next time. He is going to receive a handicapped income, because God says so!"

Eric asked; "Did God tell you that?"

I told him; "Jesus said in John 15:7 "IF YOU ABIDE IN ME AND MY WORDS ABIDE IN YOU ASK WHAT YOU DESIRE AND IT SHALL BE DONE FOR YOU."
Do you believe that?

Eric smiled and continued; "THEN THESE SIGNS WILL FOLLOW THOSE WHO BELIEVE."

We held hands and prayed together for victory in Jesus' name. When they called for Monsieur Leduc, Eric and I entered the room. It was a big room that looked more like a place to judge criminals than a place for helping hands. Twelve men were seated on an elevated platform with a long desk before them. In the middle was a big red velvet armchair in which sat the president of the Cotorep, it was impressive.

The president said; "Excuse me, but we asked for Monsieur Leduc."

Obviously, Eric did not look like "Monsieur Leduc" he was 12 years old.

I said; "Yes! I am his voice because Leduc is in the hospital. Here is the file from the hospital and a letter from the doctor."

Then I took a recorder out of my purse and pushed the record button at which all the men jumped out of their chairs.

One old man with an angry face said; "What are you doing? It is forbidden to record anything in this room, put that thing away immediately."

I got a feeling that most of them were atheists or communists. I put back the recorder in my purse but did not shut it off.

And said; "The reason I wanted to record this meeting was for Leduc to hear that you care about his condition, that he is a human being and that he has the right to exist like you and me."

Another man asked: "Who are you? Why are you involved in his case, are you a social worker?"

I was asking God to give me the right answer and to put words in my mouth.

I said: "I am a single mother of three children. My husband disappeared in the mountains of Switzerland nine years ago.
I found Leduc on a road with a broken leg; I took him to the hospital. He came out of "La Dass" the government orphanage that threw him out when he turned 18. He does not have a family and because of his health, every time he gets a job, something breaks in his body......
Why do I take care of him? Can you imagine that by a tragic accident your child became an orphan and was put in "La Dass". I thought this could very well be my son's story. I hope you would also care. If you read the medical report, you will see that you can do something for him."

They inspected his file then talked together.

The President addressed me; "I am sorry but those files are not sufficient to put him into our system. This meeting is adjourned."

I exclaimed; "Excuse me! I thought "LA COTOREP" was a humanitarian organization, but you are just a robotic organization pretending to be human. If a person does not correspond to a number in your system, you refuse him because of a piece of paper?"

An ugly older man interrupted me;

"Nobody told you to pick up that guy. You are not responsible for him!"

I answered; "Oh Yes! We can pick up cats and dogs because we have a SPA (Society Protecting Animals.) who cares, no paper requirement for them. What about a human being dying on the road? The normal response is to help someone in distress."

The president and all the men started laughing.

I was furious; "Oh yes this makes you laugh because you eat every day and sleep in a good bed every night. If you don't take consideration of this man, I am going higher."

The president; "Please excuse us Mrs. Hinman, I did not mean to be insensitive, it is just the way you said for dogs and cats, there is the SPA. I am going to make an exception for your protégé. We will take more consideration for his case. You can go now."

I told him; "No I am not leaving this room without something in writing in my hands. You must give me a paper with a confirmation of what you just said, signed by you Mr. President."

With a smile the president stood up and told his secretary, who was in the room, to give Mrs. Hinman what she asked for in her office.

In her office, the secretary told me; "There was fire in you, something out of this world. I am Christian and I saw God in you. Bravo!"

It was late. Eric and I went out to eat to celebrate the victory in JESUS!
YES! And everything was on my recorder.

Chapter 23

AGAINST ALL ODDS

The French government started asking for birth certificates for children going to school. None of my children were born in France and none of them had a French father. Esther was born in 1967 in Bern, Switzerland. Eric in 1969 was born in Rome Italy and Nouchka in 1974 in Montreal, Canada. They were all three on my passport under Russell's last name, Hinman.

I went to the American embassy to ask for a certificate of death for Russell in order for them to have French nationality. The ambassador could only give me a paper signed for the date that Russell was missing nine years ago.

The French government would not give my children French nationality unless I had a death certificate for their father.

I went back to the American embassy and explained our issue to the American Ambassador. He gave me three American passports for the children but not for me since Russell never unregistered me in the embassy in Switzerland.

After we got married, we never wanted to go to America anyway. The Ambassador told me for the sake of my children, I needed to go to America and find some relative for my children to have the opportunity to have an education and make a life for themselves.

We did not know anyone in USA. I did not want to go to America but my children's future was more important to me than me.

I was not well. In France I had free medical care and financial support for my children. Esther was recognized as a rising talented

singer composer. My Ballet School gave us extra income. We were comfortable in that place with a lot of artist friends.

I prayed; "Lord I will do what you tell me to do, I know tribulations are getting worse, many missionaries are tortured to death. Please Lord, protect my children, I need You Lord."

God's word came to me very strongly;

"GREAT SHALL BE THE PEACE OF YOUR CHILDREN. IN RIGHTIOUSNESS YOU SHALL BE ESTABLISHED. YOU SHALL BE FAR FROM OPPRESSION AND FROM TERROR FOR YOU SHALL NOT FEAR. FOR IT SHALL NOT COME NEAR YOU."

Every day, I continued to seek the Lord for direction. Then one day, God gave me this scripture;

"FOR THE LORD YOUR GOD IS BRINGING YOU INTO A GOOD LAND, A LAND OF BROOKS OF WATER, OF FOUNTAINS AND SPRINGS, THAT FLOW OUT OF VALLEYS AND HILLS. A LAND OF WHEAT AND BARLEY. A LAND IN WHICH YOU WILL LACK NOTHING. (Deuteronomy chap. 8)

According to Daniel's prophesy, the great tribulation will start in the Middle East. Israel will be encircled by the whole Muslim world. Their agenda is to kill all the Jews, wipe out Israel from the map, then all the Christians and then all who will not convert to be a Muslim.

It was evident that America will not suffer much in comparison to Europe.

France was already invaded by Muslims and Muslim families were reproducing seven to ten children. All of them are taught from birth to be a "JIHAD".

I entered the study room and announced to the children;

"We are going to America!"

The children lifting their heads from their study said; "When?"

I answered; "As soon as God provides plane tickets and the 2000 dollars required by the American law."

I put out a sign. "EVERYTHING FOR SALE MOVING OUT OF THE COUNTRY."

Shortly all our needs were met. Before buying the plane tickets; Esther and Eric were talking;

"If Russell is dead, why are we going to America? We don't know anyone in America, and it is such a big country where are we going? Omar is not dead and Nouchka never met her dad, why not go to Montreal?"

"I thought for a moment, it was so painful, I never talked to my children about my broken heart. I needed to be strong and courageous in front of them. But it was sometimes so hard.

To talk about Omar was to have my wounded heart bleeding again. I admired my children for not resenting him after abandoning us when we thought I only had a few months to live. All the sorrow they went through.

They wanted so much to have a father in their lives. They just forgave him. Now 8 years later I was alive, only depending on the power of the blood of Jesus Christ, He was my daily medicine; I claimed His word every day;

"Jesus, you give me the authority to use Your name, therefore I bind and cast down spiritual wickedness of this world and render them harmless against my children and me in the mighty name of Jesus Christ! (Matthew 18:18)"

I CAN DO ALL THINGS THROUGH CHRIST WHO STRENGTHENS ME (Phil.4:13).

Looking at their anxious faces, I agreed with them; "OK we are going to Canada."

=========================

We arrived in Montreal in December 1983. We stayed in a Motel, and then my son insisted for me to find Omar's phone number in a phone book. I was calm outside, for my children's sake, but trembling inside.

Omar answered the phone. I told him his eight-year-old daughter wanted to meet him. He asked for the address and he came immediately with his wife and his 3 children. He and his wife insisted for us to come, stay in their home.

Their two-story house was in the wealthy section of Montreal. Nouchka was radiant with joy, hugging and kissing her father. The resemblance with her father was shocking; she looked more like him than his other children.

Esther and Eric kept silent and stayed in a corner not knowing what to say after so many years. Celine, Omar's wife was very nice; she was a nurse in a hospital. She told Esther and Eric that they could stay with mom and live in their home for as long as they wanted.

Omar said; "Yes, you are all my children and the house is big enough for everyone."

They asked Esther to play for them. Esther always had her guitar who was her loyal companion since Omar taught her to play when she was six years old.

Esther started to sing a song she wrote (in French) with my help, that said;

"WHEN I WILL LEARN TO FORGIVE THOSE THAT HURT ME (with her eyes closed and tears rolling down her face.) WHEN I WILL LEARN TO FORGIVE THOSE WHO ABANDONED ME, THEN I WILL BE ABLE TO SAY I LOVE YOU, LORD."

Celine was wiping her tears. Omar was speechless. He hugged Esther and Eric with emotion and he finally said;

"I cannot change the past but I can do something now. I will be your father and we will live here all together."

I was wandering if that was why God guided us there because I was not well and had very bad days. A week later I got sicker. I prayed asking God if this was the kind of life He had for them so I could go in peace to my heavenly home.

I observed Esther and Eric were hurt watching the other children getting all of Omar's attention. I thought...No! Not on my watch, as long as I am on this earth, I WILL hold the Lord's hand and I will take care and love my children.

I was with my last seventeen hundred dollars. I went to a used car dealership and bought a large Pontiac, negotiating it to seven hundred dollars. That left us with a thousand bucks.

Asking nothing of Omar, I packed our belongings and said goodbye and thanked them for their hospitality.

Omar said; "The only thing I can offer you is our hospitality, after you are gone don't expect anything from me."

December 15th, 1983, we arrived in Quebec. We went to the big "Mall" of the town, to be warm and to witness.

One middle-aged couple was watching. Esther singing two songs and when the people came around, I will talk about salvation in the blood of Jesus Christ with some story of recent people that converted.

This couple introduced themselves as Rene and Jeanne, and said; "Last night while reading our Bible, we prayed and the Lord touched our hearts when we asked Him, Lord, who do you want us to bless? Then the Lord gave us (2John1:2)

TO THE ELECT LADY AND HER CHILDREN WHOM I LOVE IN TRUTH AND NOT ONLY I BUT ALSO ALL THOSE WHO HAVE KNOW THE TRUTH BECAUSE OF THE TRUTH WHICH ABIDES IN US AND WILL BE WITH US FOREVER.

Today when we listened to your daughter singing about the word of God, we just knew God was talking to us about you."

Our first night in Quebec our heavenly Father, provided a nice home to rest.

Rene and Jeanne hosted us. They were charismatic Catholics and introduced us to Monseigneur Lavoie, and together they had Esther on Canadian national TV, singing with her own composition. People were very impressed by this talented teenager. Monseigneur Lavoie was a Cardinal, a revolutionary charismatic priest, always opposing openly the wrong doing of the government and criticizing the church for its apathy. His picture and commentary, was a weekly appearance in the local newspaper and TV.

In Quebec, they speak French and it was a beautiful town with all the lights of the Christmas decorations and the snow. Monseigneur Lavoie hosted us in his big home. He loved our radical approach to witnessing and wanted us to go with him to every public meeting, giving us the podium so we could witness to everyone in business places and in homeless shelters.

Nouchka will get up every morning by herself at 5 am to accompany Monseigneur to the Nun Covent, bringing communion to them in the freezing morning. Monseigneur Lavoie was so delighted and all the Nuns cherished her devotion. Little Nouchka would not miss that for anything, Nouchka loved to be his helper, holding the communion ceremony. Monseigneur Lavoie had a little lump between his eyebrows that looked like a ring bouton doorbell, and

Nouchka would push it with her finger and said "Dring! Dring! time to go!"

Monseigneur Lavoie was surprised that I did not have baptism certificates for my children so he decided with our accord, to baptize them.

After Christmas, I got very sick again, the winter was brutal for me.

It was time to move to some place where the sun shone. We packed up again and drove from Canada to Florida, sleeping and eating in the car.

Chapetr 24

MIAMI

When we arrived in America, I needed to use only our passport names. I was at the end of our financial resources just $20 left. I stopped at a cafeteria where policeman was having coffee with donuts. I talked to one of them and asked if he knew a place for us to stay for the night for less than $20. The policeman was very nice, he said we needed much more than that in 1983. He talked on his car phone with other policemen.

Then he said; "Follow me I will take you to the Salvation Army. They will have food and a clean bed for all of you as long as you need."

We were happily surprised, the Salvation Army had a nice new building to host people, like woman in probation from the prison. Prison can be an establishment, or we can be prisoner from our past. I had to focus on the Lord to be free from my past.

Salvation Army had a large parking lot, where we parked the car, with all our belongings in it.

The next day we wanted to take the car to go to the Governor of Miami to make some research about Russell's family. When we opened the door of the car, we discovered that all our belongings were stolen, including Esther's albums.

Welcome to America! We found very fast it was not only rich American in Florida, but a lot of people in need in Miami.

The Salvation Army accepted our volunteer services.

JARL WAHLSTRÖM
GENERAL

ANDREW S. MILLER
TERRITORIAL COMMANDER

The Salvation Army

FOUNDED IN 1865 BY WILLIAM BOOTH

DIVISIONAL HEADQUARTERS
FOR
FLORIDA
3101 LAKE ELLEN LANE
TAMPA, FLORIDA 33618

LT. COLONEL MARO SMITH
DIVISIONAL COMMANDER

MAILING ADDRESS:
P.O. BOX 270848
TAMPA, FLORIDA 33688
TELEPHONE
(813)962-6611

January 23, 1984

Esther Hinman
Miami, Florida

Re: Future Officers' Fellowship
Luncheon - Youth Councils -
Saturday, March 24, 1984

Dear Esther:

You are invited to the Future Officers' Fellowship
Luncheon at Youth Councils on Saturday, March 24, 1984.

I do hope you will be able to attend. A reservation has
already been made with the hotel for you.

Should you NOT be able to attend please let me hear from
you immediately.

Thank you and God Bless you.

Yours in Christ,

Captain John H. Bledsoe
DIVISIONAL YOUTH SECRETARY
FLORIDA DIVISION

JHB/jf
xc: Major Thomas Woodcock

Esther would sing for the youth conventions and I would go with the
Captain and the Marshall to their business meeting for raising funds
for the needy. Every time they took me with them, they came back

with two times more money than when they went by themselves. The captain surnames me "Mary Poppins."

I was not able to get a green card, in exchange for working for them, they provided an apartment in Miami Beach, and all the furniture and filled up our fridge every week.

GOD BLESSES THE SALVATION ARMY!

The children went to school. Esther after school worked 3 hours at a Jewish sporting clothing store. Eric worked at Publix as a bagger he would go fishing in the Ocean with just a stick of wood and an old fishing line that some fisherman threw away. He often came back with a plastic bag full of fish.

Eric said; "I am the man of the house. I must put food on the table!'

I went to ask the Social Security Office for Widows benefit. After checking Russell's record, they said I cannot have it because my husband was not dead.

I was speechless. After all the research the American Consulate did, they never looked for the S.S.O.

After 12 years, I myself had to discover that my husband was still alive. I asked them for his address but they told me they are forbidden to give anyone the address from the S.S.O. I explained that I came from France with my children and asked if I write a letter would they be able to forward it to him.

After talking to their superior, they accepted to do that.

I received a letter from Boston Russell lawyer, asking me to sign divorce papers. Russell's address and phone number was on the papers that I was given to sign. I called Russell. He asked how I got his unlisted phone number and I told him from his lawyer and that his children would like to see him. He told me he will not see them until I sign the divorce papers. I did and then Esther went to Boston to visit her father. She had a very nice time with him.

He told Eric he will see him after he will come back from a business trip in Italy. There he married a lady 30 years younger than him, he was 66 and she was 36 years old.

He never invited Eric to visit him because he left for Honolulu with an offer to restoration of the art of the Iolani Palace.

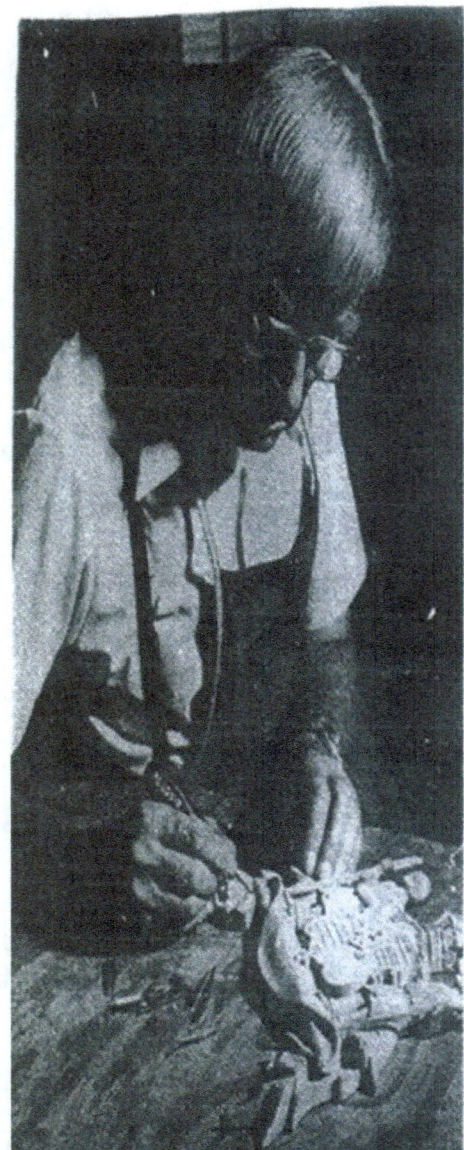

Schwamb Mill wood sculptor Russell Hinman works on
ıl Hawaiian coat of arms for 'Iolani Palace, Honolulu, where
inal furnishings are being recreated for the Throne Room
toration Project in the palace of the kings of Hawaii.

*"Man has a real hunger for quality.
It is something that is lost in this
mechanized time. Machines can carve
what I am doing but something is lost."*

— *Russell Hinman*

Old Schwamb Mill Master Carve

Brookstone Craftsman News

Russell Hinman with a coat of arms for a frame.

The n
provides space for master carver
Hinman, a man cut from the old
truly dedicated European carver

"Man has a real hunger for qi
said Hinman. "It is something tha
in this mechanized time. Machin
carve what I am doing but some
lost. The texture isn't the same.

At the moment Mr. Hinman
pleting a series of coat of ar
carved in wood by hand. Each
arms will be set on top of a case
from each respective country.
Jewels are part of a collection th
ınged to the monarchy of Hav
on be on exhibition in H
els, however, are all in
carving is being done

The coats-of-arms are being hand-
carved by Russell Hinman, an American sculptor/painter/woodcarver who
trained and worked 26 years in Europe
before returning to this country. Each
coat-of-arms will take 150 to 200 hours
from plank to finished work—not count
ing the gessoing and gilding. The one
surviving original Hawaiian coat-of-
arms is being restored.

In a way, it's almost poetic: a restored
and preserved mill working to help restore and preserve another part of

USA 10c

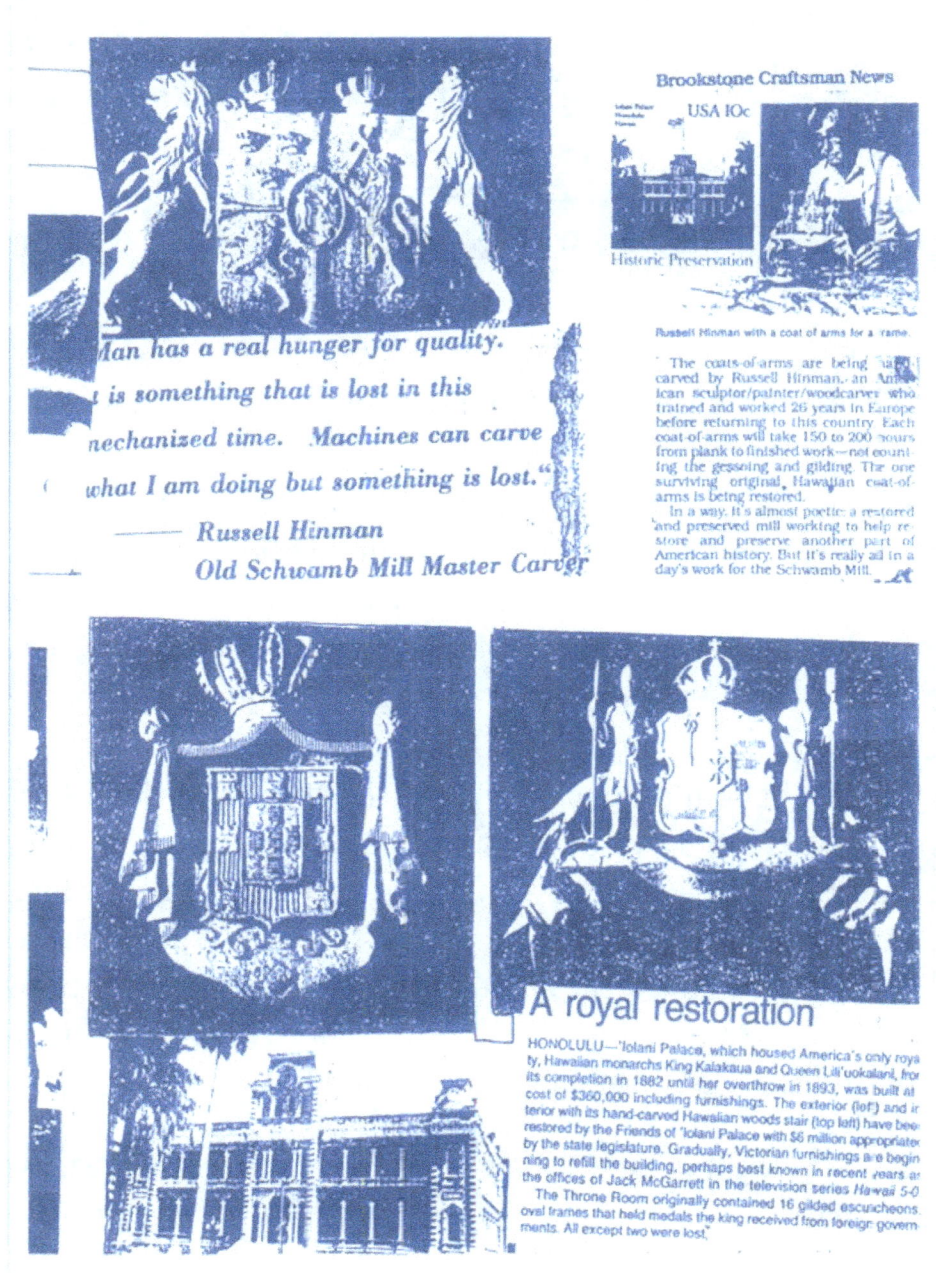

Man has a real hunger for quality. It is something that is lost in this mechanized time. Machines can carve what I am doing but something is lost."

—— Russell Hinman
Old Schwamb Mill Master Carver

Brookstone Craftsman News
USA 10c
Historic Preservation

Russell Hinman with a coat of arms for a frame.

The coats-of-arms are being hand carved by Russell Hinman, an American sculptor/painter/woodcarver who trained and worked 26 years in Europe before returning to this country. Each coat-of-arms will take 150 to 200 hours from plank to finished work—not counting the gessoing and gilding. The one surviving original Hawaiian coat-of-arms is being restored.

In a way, it's almost poetic: a restored and preserved mill working to help restore and preserve another part of American history. But it's really all in a day's work for the Schwamb Mill.

A royal restoration

HONOLULU—'Iolani Palace, which housed America's only royalty, Hawaiian monarchs King Kalakaua and Queen Lili'uokalani, from its completion in 1882 until her overthrow in 1893, was built at cost of $360,000 including furnishings. The exterior (left) and interior with its hand-carved Hawaiian woods stair (top left) have been restored by the Friends of 'Iolani Palace with $6 million appropriated by the state legislature. Gradually, Victorian furnishings are beginning to refill the building, perhaps best known in recent years as the offices of Jack McGarrett in the television series Hawaii 5-0

The Throne Room originally contained 16 gilded escutcheons. oval frames that held medals the king received from foreign governments. All except two were lost.

- -

Nouchka, at nine years old, started modeling for children's clothing earning $50 an hour.

My children always gave me all their pay checks for the bills and never asked for anything. They were proud to be providers for our needs.

The apartment building tower next door to us was filled with wealthy Jews that I witnessed to. Some of them asked me to be one of their caregivers, they did not care that I did not have a work permit. Ralf coming out of the hospital, after heart surgery was handicapped, he told all his friends, talking about me;

"She is my Rabbi."

Everyone in that building wanted me to be their care giver. A month later, Mrs. Rottenberg came out of the hospital; she was in very bad shape after a surgery and was not happy with the nurse the hospital gave her. She complained to Ralf about it. Ralf agreed to share me. Now I had 2 patients on the same floor to look after. After almost a month, Mrs. Rottenberg started to walk again. When she joined the meetings in the lobby, she bragged about me;

"You can ask anything of Mimi, she always says "yes", she is worth a pot of gold!"

No one in the nondenominational Christian church we faithfully attended ever wanted to give me a job because I was not able to get a green card.

Esther needed to be 18 years old to apply for me to become an American citizen. If it were not for the generosity of the Jews, we would be very poor.

"LONG LIVE THE JEWS!"

For over two years, I took care of Mrs. Rottenberg, an Austrian Jewish lady 82 years old. Mrs. Rottenberg was tall and beautiful for her age. She had a very proud, authoritarian personality.

After her husband was killed by the Nazis during WWII, she escaped Vienna and arrived in America by boat in 1945, after a detour to China.

President Franklin Roosevelt had done a pact with King Saud of Saudi Arabia for America to be their only oil buyer.

President Roosevelt was anti-Semitic and refused to help Israel or accept all the persecuted Jews from Europe. Thank God for President Harry Truman, who in 1945, opened up immigration for Jews coming to America.

Mrs. Rottenberg and I had a very close relationship, being European and educated in a strict Christian private school. I never called an older person by their first name, which was a lack of respect. She was also from the old school and appreciated my education. I pampered her, doing her make-up and hair. I also took care of her older sister who lived in the same building.

And her sister-in-law, whose daughter was so thankful for taking good care of her bedridden mother, often, sitting with her all night. One night I thought this poor lady needed some nutrition and not only to be stuffed with medication as if waiting to die. I went to the kitchen and found only garlic, flour and butter. I made her a soup with those three ingredients plus a little salt and water. It was the consistency of baby food. I put a small spoon in her mouth, she swallowed and opened her eyes, and said; "More" and ate a big bowl of soup.

The next morning the doctor came to visit, ready to sign a certificate of death, she was with me in the bathroom, I gave her a shower and put clean clothes on her, she walked out holding my arm, she was very tiny.

The doctor asked me; "What did you do?"

I told him; "Just garlic soup, she was starving."

He smiled and said; "I need some of your soup myself!"

Her daughter was so thankful; she gave me a gold ring with a big pearl surrounded by diamonds and gold earrings with real pearls. I wore them all the time, going to church I looked like a million bucks!

Mrs. Rottenberg did not want to look like she appreciated me any less than her niece, and so she gave me one pair of her precious diamond earrings. She was very generous. She bought me a plane ticket to France when my mother broke her leg. Esther replaced me as caregiver for two weeks.

Lots of people say Jews are stingy, but in my experience, they were the most caring, generous people I ever met. One afternoon Mrs. Rottenberg asked me to come and sit on the sofa after I finished to clean the Kitchen, and to relax.

She said to me; "You look pale lately, are you sick?"

I did not answer, I fainted. She called for help. The doctor was concerned and said;

"I cannot understand how you work in your condition; I can feel tumors through your skin."

The complete medical exam revealed that much of my body was occupied with malignant tumors. This was the same diagnosis by the doctor in Montreal, who predicted I would only live a few more months. But 11 years later I was still alive, only by the grace of God.

At St. Francis hospital in Miami Beach, the doctor tried not to look at me,

He said; "You must prepare your children and put your house in order, the tumors have spread all over your body. There is nothing anyone can do except to continue to pray. I am sorry."

I called my Pastor David, him and his wife Suzanne did not have any children; they loved my children and their good behaviors, they often had Nouchka stay in their home.

Pastor David along with one assistant pastor came to visit me. They helped me make my last will. Pastor David accepted with his wife the custody of my three children. I thought everything was working out for the best of my children. Esther was 18, Eric 16 and Nouchka 11 years old.

Nouchka was sleeping with me.

One morning before going to school, she kissed me and said; "I am not going to pray anymore for you to be healed, I should not be selfish, if you want to go to Jesus you can go, you don't have to suffer anymore."

My little girl said something that was so real and deep. "If YOU WANT to go to Jesus"

After she left, I felt her tears on my cheeks. I was so weak. Her voice was in my head like a broken record;
"I should not be selfish I should not be selfish" Over and over, I finally got it.

Nouchka did not want to be selfish. Then I realized I was the selfish one. I just accepted defeat.

God said; "He don't take pleasure in anyone dying."

Jesus said; "He came to give us an abundant life".

I was just accepting defeat instead of fighting back against the prince of darkness. His job is to lie and to kill. My children needed me.

I cried out; "Lord, forgive me. I am selfish, I should not give up, I know the power of your blood. Father God in the name of your precious Son Jesus the Christ who paid for all my sins and all my diseases help me not to have any more bitterness against Omar. Help me to forgive him and give me more years on earth for Esther, Eric and Nouchka until she is at least 18."

I don't know how long I prayed to God.

The room lit up... A strong ray of light came upon me. JESUS came to visit me, not to take me in my heavenly home, but to heal me instantaneously. My body became so light. I started to dance, exalting the Glory of God.

For many years I was blocking my healing, by holding resentment against Omar. The next Sunday in church, I gave my testimony. Everybody rejoiced with me giving glory to God.

Esther, 18 years old, married George also 18 years old. I did not know how to manage without Esther, it was like losing my right arm.

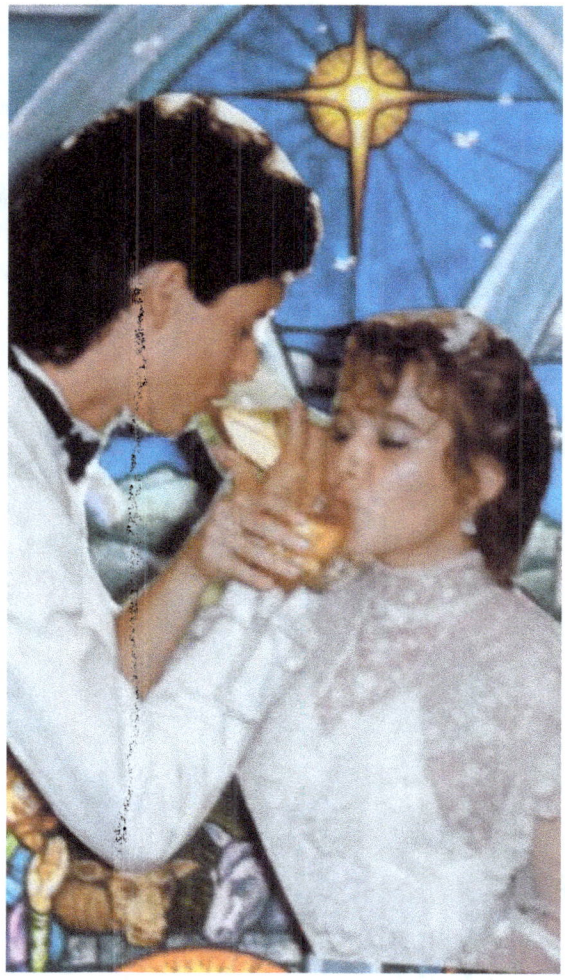

George's mother also wondered about how those two would carry on in marriage being so young, but the years have shown that they are still in love after 39 years, like "Romeo and Juliet" Happy parents of one daughter and grandparents of two lovely girls.

PSALM 116:8 FOR YOU HAVE DELIVERED MY SOUL FROM DEATH MY EYES FROM TEARS AND MY FEET FROM FALLING I WILL WALK BEFORE THE LORD IN THE LAND OF THE LIVING.

Chapter 25

CHRISTMAS 1986

During the rehearsal of a Christmas play Nouchka was in, I was reading my Bible sitting in the empty nursery of the church, when someone walked in. I lifted up my head to answer the greeting of the man who was standing before me.

I thought to myself. "Oh no! Not this guy again."

The guy who stood in front of me wore jeans with a pink shirt, he was slim and tall, black hair and blue eyes. He was holding a newspaper with his picture and an article about him in the first page, he was proud to show it to me to prove what a successful horse trainer he was.

Ola's Horse-Sense Approach To Horse Racing

BY STEVEN LIPKE

"I don't do anything in a normal acceptable pattern. I'm not radically different, just different. Ninety per cent of the people on the track do the same things. People who are a little bit innovative and have that horse-sense do better."

The speaker is Chicago-based trainer Earl Ola.

He continues: "Any good horseman knows that each horse has to be taken and trained as an individual, and as an athlete. You have to know what one horse will respond to and what another horse won't.

You have to have horse sense. There is no luck, you have to have a feel for it.

'His other big enjoyment is taking a horse that another trainer has written off as "no good" and turning it into a winning horse, a feat that he does very successfully.

Somethings tells you what to do with an animal. If you're right, you've done well. If you're wrong, you're wrong."

Watching Earl and his way of training shows you exactly how he treats his horses as athletes. He does not believe in taking a horse straight from the stall, directly to the track and galloping. He believes in the proper warmup of the horse. He brings his horses out of their stalls under tack, but with no rider on top. They are then hand-walked one round around the shedrow. After the completion of this round, the exercise rider mounts and makes six rounds around the shedrow. Then, the horse is brought to the track.

"I don't believe that a horse that has

Earl Ola, a good trainer, a good horseman

Sincerely I did not care; I tried to find something nice to tell him.

I said; "Nice pink shirt!"

The way he stared at me made me uncomfortable. Earl fixed his eyes on my hand I was wearing the big, beautiful ring. I thought what kind of man is this? Does he think that I am rich, or does he want to steal my ring?

He looked much different than the first time we had met when his friend, a jockey at the local racetrack, introduced us at church.

That day, when Earl held my hand, his mouth opened but no words came out. It seemed that his eyes popped out of his head. I thought he must have some kind of brain damage.

From that day he would always try to talk to me, following me, staring at me, and I did my best to avoid him.

Thank God I was never alone as I was either with some church member friends or with some kids; I picked up to take to church.

But on this evening, I was trapped, only him and me in the nursery. Finally, some people started coming in for the evening service and I stood up very fast to join them.

There were a lot of single men in that church who were interested in me.

Pastor David told me; "You need to get married you need a man in your house to help you."

I laughed, "To help me do what? All the men in my life did not help me, they only drowned me. No thank you... and if you try to fix me up with someone, I will change churches."

Since that day whenever a guy went to pastor David for advice on courting me, he told them not to try.

In the spring one Sunday, Nouchka had a modeling job from 6 to 10 am.

The church service was at 11 am, we would be at church just in time for the service. That was the first time that Nouchka and me were having a Sunday alone together.

The church service ended, and Earl was standing between the two exit doors.

I noticed that for the first time in a year he was wearing a suit, and I had to admit he looked great.

He started greeting Nouchka first, so I had to stop. He invited us to go out for lunch. I tried to find an excuse for not going, but it felt strange, for the first time I did not have any kids with me, and Nouchka was enthusiastic.

She said in French; "Please maman, come on, today is our day and I would love to go to a restaurant for once with only us and him."

Reluctantly I accepted, I left our car in the church parking lot, and we went with Earl to the Romeu Cuban restaurant. The meal was delicious and surprisingly the conversation was very joyful. I was discovering a very attractive guy. After the meal, Earl took us to the racehorse, training farm where he was the manager. He put Nouchka on a horse, she really enjoyed her day.

Then he filled a bag with the farm's oranges from the grove for us to take home. He gave me his phone number and asked for my phone number. The next day Earl called, then the next, it was clear that he was interested in more than friendship. I had a good idea to discourage him, so I invited him for dinner at 7 pm the next day. I finished work at 6 pm; I made myself late on purpose.

I thought Earl would lose interest when he found that my home was overflowed with my three children, Esther's Husband, George, and their baby Michelle, along with a few other young people. I thought, He will probably find an excuse to run away.

When I got home, to my surprise Earl was there perfectly at ease talking with everyone.

He was telling my children; "The first time I saw your mother, at the very moment I shook her hand, The Lord told me clearly; THIS IS YOUR WIFE. I was in shock and speechless, I probably looked strange to your mother... But last Saturday, I asked God if that was really His voice because your mother has avoided me since last year... so last Sunday morning, The Lord told me; "PUT YOUR SUIT ON, TODAY SHE IS GOING TO LUNCH WITH YOU." And it happened!"

When he was talking, I felt my face burning; I put my head in the freezer pretending to look for something. Then I heard the phone ring, I picked it up and
Said; "Hello, Hello?"

Esther was watching me, she said; "Mom, the phone is not ringing. Are you OK?"

I said to him; "Listen, Mister Ola! I have a lot of men telling me that God said I must marry them. One pastor in France drove 600 miles to tell me that God spoke to him to marry me. If God spoke to you, He will speak to me too. I think you are very hungry for a relationship, you have Mary and Claire at the church who are single woman sitting with you at church and you are very close to Claire for a long time, so why are you after me?"
Earl said; "I did not pick you, God did. I prayed for months; Lord I am lonely, please give me the woman I need, not what I want."

I thought; "What???" Then I said; "So you want Claire but you need me?"

Earl out of balance said very fast; "I don't want Claire. I told her I don't love her, when I kiss her, I always think about you!"
I really had a bad opinion about that guy, what a WACKO!

Earl called me every day asking if God spoke to me. My answer was always "NO"and it really bothered me. Earl did not stop calling every day.

I prayed, "Lord if you want to tell me something about Earl please do so or take him out of my life.

I know that cannot be You talking to Earl, plus he has a tattoo on his arm, that is an abomination, I would never marry a man with a tattoo."

God woke me up at 4 am in the morning. I heard very loudly in my head;

"DON'T BE AFRAID TO TAKE HIM FOR YOUR HUSBAND DON'T LOOK TO THE FLESH BUT LOOK TO THE HEART."

I sat on my bed trembling from head to toe. Again, Earl called, and I told him what God told me.

I said; "So, let's do it right away."
Earl walked into Pastor David's office while I stopped at the church's bookstore. Earl asked Pastor David to perform a marriage ceremony for him.

David said; "I was watching you. I knew that you and Claire were going to end up like that!
Earl said; "No, no, I am not going to marry Claire. I am marrying Michele!"

David perplexed; "Michele who?"

Earl answered; "Michele Hinman the French lady."

David started laughing; "Yes, yes, good try Earl, so what really brings you here today?"

Just then I entered Pastor David's office and gave him a hug. David was confused he said;

"This is not a joke? I have never seen you two together before. How on earth did this happen?"

We explained to him what God said to us. He was skeptical as like many preachers think that God only speaks to them.

I told him that Earl agrees to work with me, taking kids off the streets. This would give me the legal ability to house them or adopt them.

A few days before our wedding, Pastor David was talking in church about the invasion of the "Santeria" attracting so many people with their Satanic worship.

He said; "We must pray for them to go away."

I asked him; "Yes we must pray, but also do something about it, what are you going to do?"

He did not have an answer, and then said "Just pray!"

I told Earl, The Jerusalem Bible teaches us what to do to get rid of evil spirits and demons. I told him about the story of Tobit. First, we must go there to investigate what was going on. What I liked about Earl is that he agreed with everything I wanted to do, even if it sounded crazy. We arrived in the evening service of the Santeria church.

There was a big black woman, dressed in white, in the middle of a lot of candles, smoking a cigar and drinking Rum from the bottle. She had a big knife and a live chicken near, on a table with a few glasses of water. She was making incantations for the water to move before sacrificing the chicken. We stayed in the back watching. I was praying in tongues binding the evil spirits.

She stopped and walked in the middle of the crowd.

She was now yelling "The water is not moving! There is someone here interfering with the spirits!"

Then she pointed her finger at me yelling; "She is the one!"

Two big black guys grabbed me; Earl immediately grabbed the metal chair next to him, ready to start swinging it.

"I told him stop, put it down, it's Ok"

They brought me in front of the priestess.

I started to talk very loudly; "If you think your spirit has so much power, why don't you ask it to make this boy in the wheel chair stand up and walk?"

The young handicapped boy was in the front row. The crowd was listening and someone started to push the boy in the wheel chair to the front of where we were. The big woman was talking in her language to her two body guards.

I was preaching to the crowd; "Only Jesus Christ has the power to heal you and cleanse you from all of your sins, Jesus said; "IN MY NAME YOU WILL PUT YOUR HANDS ON THE SICK AND ALL THOSE WITH INFIRMITY AND THEY WILL BE HEALED! Bring the boy to me!"
The two big guys grabbed me and threw me out with Earl. We went home.

Earl said; "Well you tried, but Pastor David is right we can only pray."

I was not in peace. I would not give up without a fight. I picked up the Jerusalem bible. I read to Earl the story of Tobit. That is also a book in The New American Bible (not in the King James and other new bible versions).

TOBIT; Chapter 6:4 "BUT THE ANGEL SAID TO HIM "TAKE HOLD OF THE FISH AND DON'T LET IT GET AWAY!"

The angel told him; "CUT THE FISH OPEN AND TAKE OUT ITS GALL, HEART AND LIVER AND KEEP THEM WITH YOU, THEY ARE USEFUL MEDICINES."

Earl was listening with his eyes closed and I suspected that he was falling asleep, and not listening.

I told him; "This is a true love story and that is what I am going to do, cast out demons, with you or without you."

Earl exclaimed, "What? What are you talking about?"

"Yes! That is all in the Bible, are you going to listen?"

Suddenly he became very interested. I read Chapter 6:14 'Tobiah objected to Azariah (he did not know he was "Raphael"God's angel) he said; I don't want to marry her, I have heard that this woman has already been married seven times. On the very night that her husband's approached her, they dropped dead; it was a demon that killed them. So now I too am afraid of this demon, because he loves her. I am my father's only child. If I died, I would bring my father and mother down to their grave in sorrow over me." The angel said to him "Remember your father commanded you to marry a woman from your own family. Now listen to me, I know that tonight you shall have her for your wife! When you go to the bridal chamber,

"TAKE THE FISH'S LIVER AND HEART, AND PLACE THEM ON THE EMBERS FOR THE INCENSE. AS SOON AS THE DEMON SMELLS THE ODOR HE WILL GIVE OFF, HE WILL FLEE AND NEVER AGAIN COME BACK."

And it all happened the way the angel of God told him.

Earl asked me; "Now what?"

I told him "let's go! Let's drive to the fisherman pier".

We arrived when people were cleaning their boat. I asked one fisherman for a big fish so I can have the liver and the heart. He gave me a big barracuda for free. I took the heart and the liver and a can with matches. Then we went back to the Santeria, outside the fenced gate.

We saw them doing their service. I put the liver and the fish heart in the can and started to burn it. The smell was strong. Someone from the inside came to alarm the people, and we took off. One week later, the news announced that the Santeria church closed down. ALLELOUIA!

Esther was Twenty years old, Eric eighteen. Nouchka, thirteen years old, had been sharing the bedroom with me for so many years and now she needed to have her own bedroom. It was very difficult for her to accept that this man will be sleeping with her mom.

Helen, Earl' mother, came for a week before the wedding. The wedding day was getting close and I started having panic attacks. His mother wanted to buy me a wedding dress so we went to the mall and all the dresses I saw were beautiful but it felt all too exaggerated. They were catered young brides and not relevant for a 47 years old grandmother... what a waste of money. What I needed was a new set of pots. Not a frivolous expensive wedding dress. I would make my dress. Helen got us the pots and I went to buy white satin fabric and cobalt blue fabric for 15 dollars and made a long blue dress for Nouchka and a two pieces long white satin dress for me. It is more my style.

Earl was also 47 years old. He was a veteran from the US Marine and had spent 2 years in Lebanon, from 1958 to 1960 during President Eisenhower Blue Bat war in Lebanon.

Earl was a native of Riverside Illinois. He had a BS degree in science and multiple degrees in computer and accounting. He was an international adventurer, hunter of crocodiles for their skins in Australia. He also trapped venomous live snakes so laboratories could produce anti-venom. He lived in the jungle for two years with another crazy young man John.

He also traveled many countries and learned the different ways they were training race horses in order to become a successful horse trainer. After his last divorce he came to Miami to start a new life. Earl told me about his previous life. I was not enthusiastic about it... in the contrary; I questioned God if that was really Him who told me to marry him.

Chapter 26

WEDDING DAY

The wedding day was here. I was trembling and not able to breathe having another panic attack. Suzanne, the pastor wife, tried to calm me down.

She said; "Michele, this is not the first time you are getting married, what is wrong with you?"

I murmured; "That is why!"

But that was the first time I had a real marriage ceremony, legally and in the church. A commitment to life. During the ceremony Pastor David asked me to repeat after him, I was shaking so hard, I was not able to articulate a word. I just moved my lips.

All my friends came for the wedding along with Earl's mother, Mrs. Rottenberg, my two French friends, Chantal and Martine, the English couple, Richard and Sandra and some friends from Estonia and Cuba and of course my children with George and baby Michelle my first grandchild, and my church family.

That was May 16, 1987, after 13 years of being a single mom. Earl's mother asked her son why I was trembling.

Earl told her; "Because she is scared!"

She asked; "Scared of what?"

Earl's answer was; "Of me, because of her previous marriages, she does not trust men."

FOR THE LORD GOD IS OUR SUN AND OUR SHIELD HE GIVES US GRACE AND GLORY.THE LORD WILL WITHHOLD NO GOOD THING TO THOSE WHO DO WHAT IS RIGHT. (PSALM 84:11)

Reflecting on those days, God's amazing grace! You are so good to me Lord, my heart is moved with thanksgiving, for giving me a faithful man, who still after all these years, looks at me with so much love, that it is so embarrassing in public, he makes me blush. I am so glad that I trusted God, despite my feelings and judgment.

Earl had three beautiful daughters living in Australia, from a previous marriage. I had the great pleasure to meet the three of them, when we were invited for Mardi's wedding, his youngest daughter. We are in good communication with them despite the distance.

THERE IS NO FEAR IN LOVE, BUT PERFECT LOVE CASTS OUT FEAR, BECAUSE FEAR INVOLVES TORMENT. BUT HE WHO FEARS HAS NOT BEEN MADE PERFECT IN LOVE. (1 JOHN 4:18)

The first week of our marriage, Earl and I were walking in the street in Miami Beach. There was a drunken homeless guy on the floor who was asking for money for food.

I told him we are taking you home with us we will feed you and help you.

Earl looked at me very concerned, the guy smelled very badly. That was not the kind of honey moon he had in mind.

I told Earl; "We need to help him. He is a creation of God. Who knows what tragic situation he went through to end up like this?"

Jesus said; "WHATEVER YOU DO TO THE LEAST OF THOSE YOU DO UNTO ME"

My husband said; "I cannot imagine Jesus being drunk and smelling this bad."

We brought him home in our car to feed him.

Earl said; "We need to bring him to my friend's farm to work in the barn and to sleep there."

I said; "Ok, but first he needs a shower and clean clothes."

The man was so drunk so I said I was going to take him in the shower to scrub him down.
Earl freaked out.
He said; "No way! I am going to give him the shower!"

Earl, in his swimming suit, was taking the man's clothes off of him. They were sticking to his body's open sores. Earl had never had such a disgusting situation like that happening to him in all his life. The smell was so bad; it was a real challenge to go through with this task.

He prayed; "Please Lord help me not to vomit on this poor man."

Suddenly he felt a heavenly presence near him and all the discomfort disappeared. Something changed in his spirit and he felt a Godly love that touched him deeply with compassion. He came out of the bathroom; the man was clean, shaved and new clothes. Earl's face was so different. Something happened to him, his eyes were shining with the Holy Spirit. The Lord sent an angel to help him.

Chapter 27

THE MENNINGER FOUNDATION

Mrs. Rottenberg moved into her new, exclusive assisted living facility, where I visited her every day. The Menninger Foundation was advertising in the Miami newspaper about their need married couple for parenting abused children. Earl and I went for an interview and were accepted.

We started an intensive training program with psychologists.

The training we received was to learn how to handle problem children. Some of them came from juvenile prisons or mental hospitals and most of them had drug dealer parents who sold them for sex trafficking to satisfy their drug addictions.

The Menninger Foundation was established by an American family who had been practicing psychiatry since 1862. They were dedicated to research, training, and public education. Religion was well accepted and they observed that people who believed in Jesus recovered faster than those who did not.

We began the journey to be foster care parents for 6 children from ages 8 to 17. We prayed over those children and read the Bible with them daily.

I also used expressive corporal dance (emotional body expression) and drama to help them move through and express their emotions. After a few months, I trained them to perform for nursing homes. Their minds were active, competing with one another; they forgot they wanted to kill somebody or themselves.

After a couple of years, I realized Earl was really the right man for me and for those kids. He was able to handle very difficult situations when things could have gotten out control. He was perfect for the job. He had the strength and natural authority to be a leader for them.

They had never before been accepted in a normal society because of too much trauma in their young lives, resulting in their inability to learn.

Every day Earl would sit for hours with those kids, teaching them that God does not create mistakes and that they could succeed. He tutored them with their schoolwork. All of them were able to pass exams to be accepted in normal schools.

God used Earl in a mighty way in the lives of those lost souls. I would never have been able to do it without him. Together we housed and rehabilitated many badly abused 27 teenagers.

Sunday and Wednesday we went to a church called "Voice for Jesus".

The Pastor, Wayne Cochran, used to be a star in show business and became a preacher after a radical conversion. He opened a church, using his voice for Jesus, and many talented singers from the show business came to join him.

All the children we had loved going to that church. It was nothing compared to a normal church and was more like a theater where people got healed, some had visions, some had words of knowledge the Bible was alive. It was fantastic!

We also had a few kids that came from Jewish backgrounds and so we took them to a Jewish Temple on Saturdays. Jesus is the Jewish Messiah.

We taught them without the Jews, we would not have salvation therefore we would't have Christians on the earth and that we must love the Jews because God chose them to bring the good news of salvation to all creation.

God said about his chosen people; "FOR HE WHO TOUCHES YOU TOUCHES THE APPLE OF MY EYE" (Zechariah chapter 2)

The Lubavitcher Rabbi, after many meeting with Earl, did an adult BAR MITZVAH ceremony in the Hassidic synagogue for Earl that is where he got his Bible name, "Abraham" because he had become a father figure to so many children.

I rejoiced with him for it was a big step, to forget the past and be a man of God. He was very serious about it. I also liked to call him Abraham better than Earl, because with my French accent, my pronunciation never came out very good with E A R L.

Esther, George and baby Michelle lived in Kendall. We moved to a big new house with a pool, with all the kids not far from them.

Eric stayed in our condo on the beach where he worked as a lifeguard. Nouchka 14 became physically sick out of fear, at the public school that she was attending. Many kids at her school were harassing her. I decided to put her in a private Christian school. Nouchka was an A student.

After the summer vacation, Abraham and I were investigating local Christian schools. We found that all of them were extremely expensive, plus their acceptance criteria were so rigid that you had to ask yourself if these were really Christians. It seemed money was their most important criteria.

One week before summer vacation ended, on our way home, we found ourselves in front of a beautiful campus called St. Brendan Catholic School.

Nouchka said; "Oh mom, that is the most beautiful school I have ever seen, I want to go to this school!"

I asked Abraham to stop the car and went with Nouchka inside the main office. The person in charge of enrolment told us there was a two-year waiting list. I asked her to speak to the principal and was told he was in a conference. The building campus was over crowded with people.

We left and Nouchka was so disappointed.

Abraham asked "what happened?

I told him about our short meeting.

He said; "Let's go see another one."

I told him; "No that is the school Nouchka wants, that is the school she will attend."

Abraham, with a questioning tone, asked;
"Din't the secretary tell you there was a two years waiting list?"

I told him; "What she said does not matter, God is Nouchka's Father. He loves her, she is going to that school next week."

Abraham puzzled; "How is that going to happen?"

I answer; "Just watch"

The next day I arrived at the school at 8 am, just in time to see the principal ready to enter his office. I ran through the middle of the school crowd and put myself between the principal's office door and him.

I said; "Please Father, give me just five minutes. It is very important. The life of a child depends on you."

Intrigued, the principal agreed to listen. I explained to him that from the time Nouchka was born, she belonged to God. That Nouchka never complained during difficult times, that she had been on the mission field with me since she was five months old. The last year in public school, she had become physically sick from fear as she was bullied for not succumbing to peer pressure.

Father Mc Grave said; "I really wish I could help you, but all our classes are already full. I don't have an opening."

I told him; "Jesus said; "I will not refuse anyone who comes to me!" Father, I believe in miracles and I know God can make a way. Please will you ask God to tell you what to do?"

The principal said; "Yes I will."

The next day, nothing, and the day after came but still no phone call from the school. Abraham lost faith about Nouchka going to Saint Brendan. To help the atmosphere, I decided to call the school, and after insisting finally I was put through to the principle's secretary.

The secretary said; "Are you Mrs. Ola? I am so glad you called because I was not able to find your phone number, please come to the school immediately to register your daughter, we had one last minute student cancellation."

WE WALK BY FAITH NOT BY SIGHT!

JEREMIAH 33:3. "CALL TO ME AND I WILL ANSWER YOU."

ABRAHAM BACK TO HORSE RACING

After seven years, Abraham and I retired from taking care of abused children due of a number of attacks from secularists and anti-Christian rules in the child care system, forbidding us to continue reading the Bible, go to church and pray with the children.

One anti-Christian social worker put charges against us. It landed us in court. Abraham applied to every Christian legal service, but he could not find assistance. While not one Christian lawyer or legal service offered assistance, a Jewish lawyer took our case even though he was not a Christian, he believed we should be honored and not persecuted for the work we had done.

It was such a hard time for me I started having panic attacks again.

The children were in despair, telling the director of the establishment they wanted "Mom and Dad" But we were terminated because of this new social worker who was in charge.

I got the worse panic attack one day and Abraham was so scared, he called my son, Eric, to pray with him over me on the phone before the medic arrived. I finished in the emergency room in Boca Raton hospital. Then we moved to Eric's home for a few days.

Abraham was hired to train racehorses in Maryland by CBN 700 CLUB founder and president, Pat Robertson. He was the finest person that Abraham had ever known. Unfortunately, after a few months, Pat Robertson was forced to get out of horse racing because of incredible pressure from other pastors.

From Maryland, we moved to Ocala, I like Florida. We found a good church OCALA WORD OF FAITH that became later MEADOWBROOK CHURCH, with Pastor Tim Gilligan.

After selling our Ocala residence, we bought 20 acres of land in Morriston.

After the unexpected death of Abraham's younger sister in 2004, Abraham's mother came from New York to live with us. She was 90 years old, blind and in a wheelchair after having hip surgery. Abraham was able to rebuild a sweet relationship with his mother. I became her caregiver.

Abraham had a stroke which resulted in serious heart problems.

January 18, 2006, he went through open heart surgery with complications.

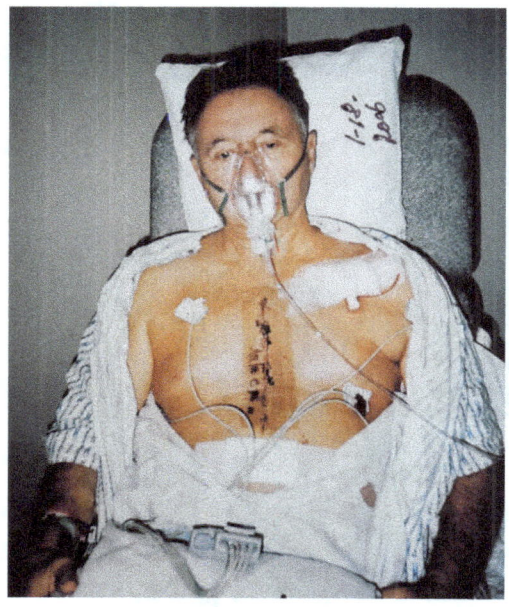

Helen, Abraham's mother, got pneumonia and was in Gainesville hospital. Abraham was in Inverness hospital, opposite directions from Morriston. I would drive every day to see my husband and pray with him then drive back to minister to Helen.

Helen never fully recovered, they put feeding tubes in her stomach and she was deteriorating very fast. Helen died March 15, 2006. She was 92 years old.

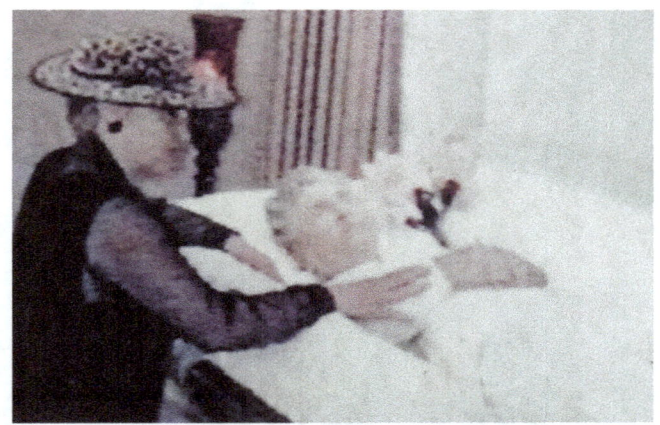

At the hospital where Abraham was, most of the other heart surgery patients went home after five days. After 10 days I was ready to take my husband home. I found Abraham's room empty on the floor nurse told me he was rushed to the emergency for a blood transfusion. He had developed emboli in his arm and leg and had contacted a serious infection in the hospital.

For quite a long time after, Abraham was not able to do anything. For a man like him who was always so strong, it was hard to believe something like that could happen to him.

He decided to sit at his computer and write for THOROUGHBRED TIME HORSES magazine, and ARABIAN RACINC illustrated.

ANGLO-ARAB RACEHORSES

By Earl "Abraham" Ola

Try to register an Anglo-Arab, or a Register of Merit Quarter Horse, as a Thoroughbred with our American Jockey Club. DNA testing is part of their registration process. It should be part of the registration process of every breed of horse, especially Arabian horses.

Anglo-Arabs are being registered as purebred Arabians in the USA. This is happening ONLY because our American Arabian Registry and our American Arabian Jockey Club have not made DNA testing part of the American Arabian registration process.

Let's take a look at Anglo-Arab racing overseas. In most countries they call all their Anglo-Arabs, Anglo-Arabs; with the exception of one European country.

This country has a Jewish President, who will not admit he is Jewish, is more pro Palestinian, pro Arab, and anti Israel than any major political leader I know of. Their politicians have criticized our war against terrorism, more than any

other European country. They say we have over reacted to September 11th. I trained one of their bloodstock agents, how to select racing prospects for his international clientele, and got him his first million-dollar sale. He ended up screwing me out of a lot of money. He is now THE most successful buyer of Thoroughbred racehorses.

Next to America I love this country more than any other. I love their horse racing, all breeds and I love their people. We should have racing like theirs. The love of my life and mother of my children comes from this country. She was Europe's prima ballerina before retiring to be a missionary in Europe and the Middle East. She is responsible for successfully raising our kids, and talking me into raising 27 foster children. We have a home in this country. This country, like ours, has opened their doors, hearts, and pockets to the world. If I had to live on welfare, I would much rather live there. They provide almost luxury apartments and a living wage to their

welfare recipients, most of whom are from the Middle East, and who cause 95% of the violent crime in their nation.

The Japanese race Anglo-Arabs at their class 2 tracks. When I worked in Japan, Anglo-Arabs accounted for almost half of the races at their class 2 tracks. Because of the unbelievable purse moneys now available to Thoroughbreds at their Class 1 tracks, the Japanese seem to have lost interest in class 2 and Anglo-Arab racing, and this part of their racing industry is in decline.

In the United Kingdom (England), like in America, Arabian racing has not really taken off. It is run by two racing associations that compete and fight against each other, and is mainly an amateur industry, except for their international races. Purebred Arabs and real Anglo-Arabs compete against each other in most races. We should work with the Brits to establish successful and unique Arab racing and betting.

The French government has top

26

Chapter 29

THE POWER OF PRAYER

Abraham's health was deteriorating. His energy level decreased dramatically and he was diagnosed with the beginning of Parkinson's and Alzheimer's disease. He also developed restless leg syndrome with joint pain.

Pastor James Watts was a charismatic prayer warrior. He opened another church just a 45minutes drive from where we live. Pastor James and all the people of the church prayed intensively over Abraham. There was dramatic improvement because of the power of collective prayer. It is called GVC, for (Grand View Church).

One morning Abraham decided to ride a horse to make sure it would be safe for his grandchildren to ride. Abraham was an excellent rider, but at 70 years old, I was worried about him riding because of his restless leg syndrome.

I tried to dissuade him with no success as usual. He was so confident that he was in control but he could not have expected a covey of quails to fly under the feet of the horse. The horse freak-out and jumped sideways right into the neighbor's electric fence and flipped over on Abraham.

1 Peter 5:8 "BE SOBER, BE VIGILANT, BECAUSE YOUR ADVERSARY THE DEVIL WALKS ABOUT LIKE A ROARING LION, SEEKING WHOM HE MAY DEVOUR."

The Lord reminded me what a missionary told me long time ago, "The devil does not go after those who do nothing for the kingdom of God to destroy them, because He already got them in his net."

I was cleaning the back porch when I heard Abraham calling me, I found him walking holding onto the horse, covered with dirt and blood. I ran to help him.

He told me; "First take care of the horse, hose him and put him in the pasture",

I did it very fast, and then helped Abraham into the shower, then into bed. He refused to go to the hospital.

He said; "I am OK, just a few bruises, it is normal to hurt, maybe a broken bone."

At evening time, I was checking on him, Abraham's body had turned black from his chest to his knees. It was obvious there was internal hemorrhaging.

Thank God Eric my son was with us.

Abraham was always more preoccupied about all our animals at the farm, he wanted me to look after them and have Eric take him to the emergency.

In Marion hospital in Ocala, after an MRI, they put him in an ambulance and sent him to Florida hospital in Orlando to the Seventh

Day Adventist hospital, which specialize in difficult injuries. They pray with the patient before operating and they extend the healing ministry of Jesus Christ.

Abraham had a broken pelvis and a fractured back along with several broken ribs. I give thanks with all my heart to my Savior, who put Pastor James and all his prayer warriors to intercede with me for my husband during those difficult times.

The doctor did not think he would be able to walk again.

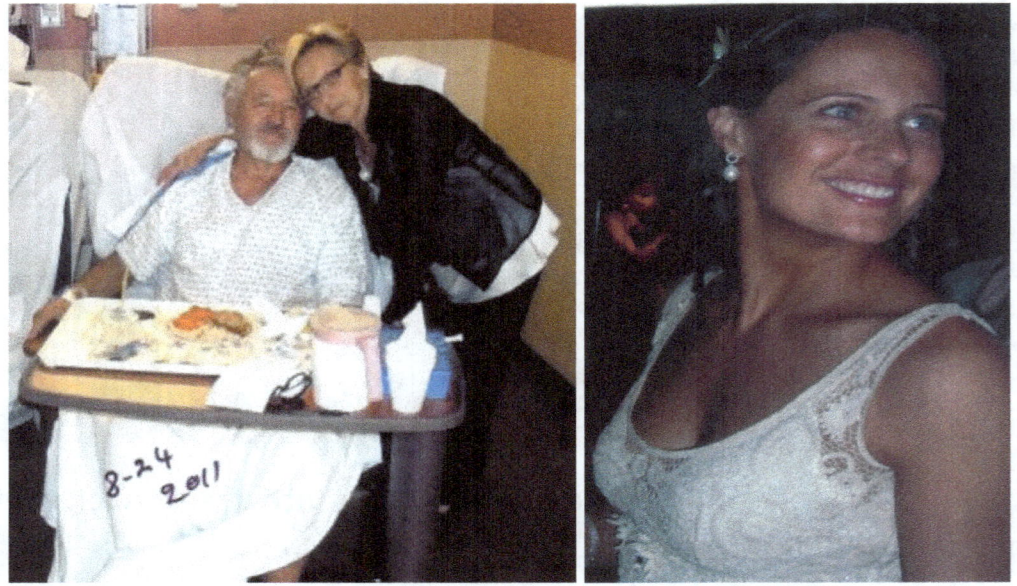

Abraham did not want me to tell his daughter and family in Australia about his accident because they were supposedly to visit at the end of the month. He was worried that they would cancel their trip.

When Mardi, her husband and their three girls arrived Abraham wanted to try his best to stand up to welcome them, with the help of a walker.

The Australian has a phrase that says most of the time "DON'T WORRY MATE!" in just about any circumstance.

They decided to take us in a tour to Disney and then to South Beach, Miami in a very nice hotel. Abraham Having a motorized wheelchair.

To have the family reunion, with Esther, George, Nouchka, Kira and Julien.

In 2013, I was not well they tested me and diagnosed me with a chronic kidney disease. The doctor wanted to put me on dialysis.

I told him "No thank you"

I run to my very best doctor of all, "JESUS"

My son Eric was very concerned about me, he insisted saying, "Mom, I will give you my kidney, you are my mother, and I want you to live longer."

I told him; "Eric, I am old you are young, and you have two little children, you need your two kidneys more than I do."

Eric said; "Listen Mom, you are going to take my kidney, I have two and if in case I need a new one, God can create a new one in me, because He is God and I believe He can do it!"

I started to laugh; "Oh yes! Just like that because you say so, but what about me?"

Eric's answer was; "I don't think you really believe God for your healing, otherwise you will not accept this disease"

I was speechless, thinking about what he just said.

I told him; "You are right, it would be much better and easier if I just trust God to heal me."

I meditated on what Jesus did for me at the cross. If I can trust God, that He gave his only son to die for my sins on the cross to have eternal life, why not believe and act on; "BY HIS STRIPES I AM HEALED?" he takes the same faith.

Eric's faith was not just a "word", he trusted God since a young age, all those years walking with God expecting and receiving miracles.

His trust did not vanish. I remembered one Saturday in 1989, when Eric was a lifeguard in Miami Beach, his captain had told me that this same day, Eric had saved five lives. The month before, he had saved a total of 37 lives all by himself.

I was astonished I exclaimed; "My son! My hero!"
Eric was embarrassed he said; "But Mom, that is my job."

During the seven years he worked there, he saved hundreds of lives. What is amazing about Eric being a lifeguard is that when he was in high school, he fainted during physical education class. The doctor said he must restrain from exercise because he had a heart murmur.
But Eric prayed according to Mark 16:17 "THESE SIGNS WILL FOLLOW THOSE WHO BELIEVE!". Eric wanted to be a lifeguard. The physical test to be a lifeguard is very strenuous with running and swimming for miles.
God healed Eric, because he believed.
God is the father of the fatherless. GLORY TO GOD!
The next Sunday we went to GVC church and Pastor James prayed a collective prayer about healing and every word that was coming out

of his mouth, he was quoting healing scriptures, touched me deeply in my soul. I was drinking every word.

The next Thursday I was back to the doctor's office to have the results of the latest tests. Everything came back normal.

The Pilipino doctor asked me. "What did you do?" Then he smiled and lifted his right arm; "I know... I know! YOU PRAYED!"

Chapter 30

LIFTED UP

After my morning devotion, I was reflecting on some boys that we had fostered and ministered to. Many people considered it a fruitless job to pray and to teach these troubled abused kids. Twenty years had passed and I was wondering if any of them had kept the faith. My heart was heavy this morning feeling worthless for the Kingdom of God. The phone rang.

A man's deep voice said; "Mommy, is that you? Yes! It is you! I know your French accent! I finally found you. I had to pay a detective to find your phone number. I am in New York."

A big question mark in my mind I asked;
"Who are you?"

"I am Lance! Your favorite boy, don't you remember me?"

I was perplexed; "Lance! Oh my! dear Lord! Lance? It's hard to believe, I was thinking about you this morning, and here you are calling after so many years. How are you doing?"

For years Abraham and me had traveled overseas in many places, it was hard to find us.

Lance said; "I am doing very good I am married and I have eight people working for me."

I asked him; "You are married to a woman?"

Lance was a black male. He had been given, by his drug addict mother, to men for sex since he was three years old so she could get her drugs. I remembered the day he started to call me "Mommy."

That day, Abraham was gone with several other kids and I was alone with Lance and Richard, another black boy. I heard shouting and fighting so I ran to their room. Lance had a baseball bat and he was yelling at Richard who had provoked him, I quickly put myself in front of Richard.

Lance Yelled to me; "Mrs. O, get out! I am going to kill this bastard, if you don't move, I will hurt you." (The children called us Mr. and Mrs. O)

I told him; "Lance, if you kill me, I am going to heaven, but you are going to hell. If you think, your life here is bad, it is nothing compared to hell where you will be tormented forever and there is no exit. Lance, I love you I don't want you to go to hell."

Since that day, something happened in his heart, and he started to call me "Mommy."

Lance had a fantastic personality, as well as Richard. I was able to make them work together doing drama plays for Easter and Christmas, showcasing their own fun personalities. When they performed, the small theater was packed and they were always a big success. That really made them feel like they were celebrities and boosted their confidence.

Lance on the phone was very excited.

He said; "Yes! I am married with a woman. I am straight, and guess what? I am the president of a program for the needy in our church. I am doing what dad and you taught me to do. I also forgave my mother. Please, if you need anything I am here for you. I am so thankful for what you poured into me. I want to tell you the work you did with dad was not in vain. I am in contact with all the boys you used to have at the cottage in Boca Raton. They all are doing well,"

Lance mentioned nine of those boys who used to be in juvenile jail.

He told me, John is married with three children, he is a lawyer, and about each one a little story.

That really melted my heart. I shared my joy with Abraham when he came back home. Abraham was amazed by the good news, and felt comforted to learn that he was the man who had sowed good seeds in the field.

Our wonderful and merciful God again orchestrated the day, to encourage us and to let us know that we should continue to put the armor of God every day and get out to kick the devil's butt.

JESUS SAID; "GO TO ALL THE WORLD AND PREACH THE GOSPEL TO EVERY CREATURE." (Mark 16:15)

Wherever we go, we are surrounded by creatures.

Chapter 31

PRIDE

In 2018, I was trying my best to hide my condition from Abraham. I was losing my balance, was experiencing weakness and the pain in my head was so extreme that it felt like it could explode. I'd fall down often, my legs getting numb and my entire left side was quite painful.

We had a very nice family doctor at the time named Naila Khan and she was a friend. Someone I could talk to and trust.

She was a Muslim and yet listened to us when we witnessed about Jesus. She even let us put Christian literature in her waiting room and every time we went to her office, she enjoyed how I demonstrated my joy in the Lord.

Abraham and I prayed over her in her office.

She invited us to her home to meet her husband and a group of her friends. She was a dear friend. She sent me for an AMR of the brain.

During Abraham's weekly doctor visit, she told him she had the results of the AMR

Doctor Naila told Abraham; "I have bad news. Michele has a brain tumor. If you told her, how she will react?"

Abraham said; "The way I know Michele, she will not be shocked, and she won't shed any tears. She will trust God like she always does."

Before coming home, Abraham went to church for the Thursday morning 11 o'clock Bible class with Mike Cureau the teacher, a dear friend of Abraham's. Abraham told him the news about me. Then all the attendants prayed for me.

Abraham came back home and told me about the test results and about the prayer meeting for me. I was not surprised about having a brain tumor, I had done some research on my symptoms before even going see doctor Naila.

We started going to The Church of God in Williston, which is only a 15 minutes' drive for us, instead of continuing our 45 minutes' drive to the GVC church.

Since Abraham's accident, I noticed my vision for driving at night was a problem. I would get lost and drive for hours just to find our private road plus I was having a lot of dizziness.

I was upset with Abraham for running to church asking them to pray over me.

I told him; "Whatever is going on in my body is between God and me. I'm not too sure I like the way they pray; "Please Lord heal Michele if that is Your will." Of course it is God's will to heal! The devil deceived and puts lies in people's minds, twisting the word of God instead of focusing on what is written;

"GOD MAY YOUR WILL BE DONE ON EARTH AS IT IS IN HEAVEN!" There is no sickness, no infirmity in heaven.

Jesus said; "I ALWAYS DO WHAT MY FATHER TELLS ME TO DO"

Jesus heals them ALL! All of those who came to him, he never said "NO" to them. Can you imagine a loving father, putting sickness on his child, to teach them a lesson? How dumb is that?"

I was brought up Catholic. Nones and monks would torture themselves as a love offering to God, like many in Indian religions and in Asia. RIDICULOUS.

There is a huge difference with what The Bible teaches us; "If we are to be persecuted for "OUR FAITH IN JESUS" great will be our reward in heaven" (MATTHEW 5: 11-12.)

Not for our diseases. I am not going back to church."

Abraham was sad at my reaction.

He said; "But Michele, they love you, why do you say those things, they really care about people, you need to accept that other people know God as much as you do. You are being too prideful."

I was mad about my condition. I was mad about people knowing about my condition. I went to my room to meditate.

The Lord snapped me into introspection. He showed me that I was reacting exactly the way I did when I was in show business... Hiding, pretending, I did not want people to pity me.

What do you call that? Oh YES PRIDE!

Abraham was right and I needed to do something about it.

The next Sunday I went to Church. I went up on stage in front of the congregation and made a public confession asking for forgiveness and asking Pastor Wess to pray over me, to cast out the spirit of pride, because it is written;

"GOD RESISTS THE PROUD BUT GIVES GRACE TO THE HUMBLE" (James 4:6 NKJV)

Abraham did not expect me to do a public confession. But I needed the grace of God more than anything, as I do every day.

I was very concerned about my husband. He had a very big health issue and needed me more than I needed him.

I prayed; "Please Lord, let him go first!" but after I prayed, he was getting better and better and I was getting worse and worse. I started to look for someone to replace me. In our church, we have many nice-looking widows that are loving and kind who was very fond of Abraham, who after all, he is a handsome looking guy for his age with a good sense of humor, great personality with extensive knowledge of religion and history.

Well, except for the heart failure and back damage etc..... He needed to have someone caring for him.

I was looking for a wife according to, Ephesians 5:22 "WIVES, SUBMIT TO YOUR HUSBANDS AS TO THE LORD."

Just like me! Yes, I failed many times but I always put him before me. I wanted the best for him, someone better than me, so he would't miss me. Abraham loves me so much he looks at me like I am so precious in his eyes, and he tells me every day that I am the best thing that has ever happened in his life. He still makes me blush, to feel so much love. What a blessing he is to me.

Abraham admired one lady in his Bible class, she was pretty, very educated and he liked her especially for her knowledge in the Bible, plus she was 10 years younger but unfortunately, she moved to another town.

Abraham did not want me to look for anyone else. Now the only good thing for him would be that I live a little longer.

I decided that it was time for me to jump out of the boat, just as Peter did when he looked at Jesus. But I needed to keep my eyes on the Lord not to the waves, no matter what the symptoms were. I was already 79 years old.

I was driving to Susan's house, a short distance from where we live, for my weekly Bible meeting when suddenly I had a terrible explosion in my head and lost control of my car. I automatically put my foot on the break, no one was on this deserted farmer road.

I started to yell; "Evil spirit of tumor, I cast you down in the name of Jesus Christ!"

This was a spiritual fight against darkness and I claimed who I was in Christ, redeemed by the blood, cleansed from sin and every sickness.

I was saying aloud; "No weapon formed against me will prosper because I am the redeemed of the Lord, tumor get out right NOW!!"

I don't remember how long I was fighting but it was a tough battle.

I then remembered what my father had taught me;

"If an enemy attacks you, never run from it, fight with all your strength until you win or die."

YES! In the name above all names, with the name of Jesus Christ I win!

I started to be possessed with the Holy Spirit of Jesus Christ with incredible joy and strength invading my soul. I was praising God all the way to Susan's house.

When I arrived, I told them what had just happened to me, all those wonderful friends were listening but I had a feeling that they thought I was weird.

A few weeks later, I testified in "The Church of God" for the first time with a praise dance with the music and the song "Amazing Grace". At 79 years old. (The Church of God never have praise dancing before)

Abraham had tears in his eyes and many women too. There was an emotional and moving standing ovation for the Glory of God. (The Church of God never allowed, praise dancing before. I convinced Pastor Wess to let me do it because it is Biblical Ps 150)

Abraham met Michelle Traylor way back in 2004 when she was the President of the Williston Library. She is so beautiful in everything she does, she is a perfectionist. I went with Abraham to the library one day, I understood why he was going there a few times a week.

When I first meet Michelle, I was surprised! To see how beautiful she was. Williston is a small town and having such a perfect, charming and Godly woman in the library, she immediately captivated my heart. And later we became best of friends and still to this day.

Her and her husband Steve came to our home to help us any way they could. Even though they lived about 20 miles away, Steve would come every week to mow our lawn.

Michelle and her sister, Charlene offered such a joyful display of God's love.

I joined the prison ministry with Charlene and we had so much fun together. She is so gorgeous and was a fashion model when she was younger. She too was going through struggles as kidney disease ran in their family and two of her daughters had to fight for their life. Charlene is also a prayer warrior and knows who she is in Christ.

A year prior she had given one of her kidneys to one of her daughters and now the other one, Sarah, needed one. Her heart wanted to give Sarah her other kidney but that was not medically acceptable. Despite all her struggles she was going through, she continued to worship and trust God. Friends like her and her sister are priceless to me.

Just few months ago, her husband Jack died. Charlene demonstrated her faith in all her trials with the hope of heaven. She never stopped to be a prayer warrior for everyone.

For my 80th birthday, my heart's desire was to have my children and my friends around me. I decided to remodel our 3 bedrooms, 2-bath guesthouse which included building an island in the kitchen area. I had 45 days to do it before the big day. I did so much by myself and Michelle came to help me to clean after I finished painting every room.

Roger, a Godly church brother, came to help me to build the island and he also built a deck on the back porch.

He still comes every Tuesday to fix anything we need to be done in our home. All those wonderful friends, come from "The church of God".

I also decided to remodel all the bedrooms in the guest house with new beds and comforters, with horse pictures and family paintings and new furniture's.

After working every day many hours running from our home to the next home, I was exhausted I went to lay down in the office bed and prayed;

"Lord, I need help to finish the guest house I am so tired."
I picked up a meditation book from Ruth Myers, on the night table, and opened without looking at page18, the scripture jumped in my eyes;

"YOU ARE PRECIOUS IN MY EYES, AND HONORED, AND I LOVE YOU" (Isaiah 43:4 RSV)

I was touched to tears and started to worship my Lord, it was evening the room suddenly lit up, and a shower of light like a myriad of diamonds came in and covered me... my soul and spirit was possessed with an incredible supernatural strength. I stood up and ran to the guess house and worked until 9 pm and continued for the next three days. Everything was done for the arrival of the family. To God be the Glory!

Sunday morning, on my 80th birthday, we all went to church. I had not told anyone, not even my husband, that I was going to give Glory to God for giving me such a long life, with so much love and blessings.

Pastor Wes said; "You did not tell Abraham that you are going to be a witness and do a praise dance?"

I answered him; "No, because Abraham is always bragging about me, and will probably tell everyone how amazing I will be. Then they all will be disappointed."

Pastor Wess was laughing.

Eric my son was nervous, he was sitting near the stage with Abraham, and his wife Ana, her son Steve, their two daughters, Elohine and Crystal. They came to visit from Colorado.

I delivered a testimony, in a comic tragic way, people were laughing and tearing.

Then I took off my long velvet black coat and shoes, and began to do a praise dance in my white dress with the song, "I LOVE THE LORD" sung by Whitney Houston (from the movie, The Preacher's Wife). What a victory in Jesus.!!! Standing ovation.

Unfortunately, my two daughters and their family did not make it. George and Esther arrived late in the afternoon.

But God gave me a big spiritual family to celebrate my miraculous healing, giving me a long life to worship Him. TO GOD BE THE GLORY

WITH LONG LIFE WILL I SATISFY HIM AND SHOW HIM MY SALVATION. (Ps.91)

PRAISE HIM WITH THE TIMBREL AND DANCE. (Psalm 150)

Chapter 32

LOVE HEALS

Abraham was in the hospital. The cardiologist told us if he performs an operation to fix the leak in his heart, it will be a 7 hours long surgery and the risks were high as he would have to stop taking blood thinner medication for seven days prior to having the surgery which could result in a major stroke. He had to make that choice. Abraham had already had an open-heart surgery in 2006 that did not go well. Abraham did not like the idea of the possible risks as well as to die in pain.

Abraham asked; "What is the alternative?

The doctor told him to use the treadmill and small weightlifting exercises starting with just few minutes a day, slowly increasing to bring oxygen to the heart to keep him alive.

Abraham was very weak, but he was determined to be able to see his children before he passed away. He forced himself to do what the doctor said. He made his way to the gym on the patio, holding on to his walker, and with all his strength continued to do all the exercises just as his doctor prescribed.

Cami being the first daughter and Jodi, Abraham's 2nd daughter, came from Australia to visit her father knowing it could be her last chance to see him. They were hugging each other, after 13 years both crying with joy.

To have his daughters with him and wanting to make them happy, Abraham forgot about himself. He started doing better each day. YES! LOVE HEALS!

We used to live on the ocean in Miami, and I loved to swim. Taking care of Abraham and living on the farm, I had a small, above ground pool, in our backyard but during the hurricane season, my pool was destroyed.

Jodi sat with her father, while they searched on the internet, to help him order a new pool. She insisted for a much bigger one. Jodi was the one who choose a rectangular pool 26 feet long, and of course Abraham agreed with everything she said.

Good for me!

I enjoyed this new pool, I started every day with a goal of 50 laps a day for a month then the next month 100 laps then the next month 150 laps, and the fourth month I was able to swim, almost every day, 200 laps, that was my goal at 80 years old.

A few months later, I woke up one morning having excruciating pain in my stomach. I went to the bathroom and blood was coming out of me. I thought maybe if I go to the pool and do my daily 200 laps, I will be OK.

But I was worse. The pain was so bad, I was not able to stay on my feet.

Abraham said; "I am calling 911"

I said; "No I need to be here to take care of you."

Abraham answered; "You need to be taken care of, you cannot do anything the way you are."

He called 911 and the paramedics came and took me to Gainesville Shands hospital.

In the ER, doctors and nurses were taking care of me and asking questions, I told them about the bleeding and the pain was worse after swimming my 200 daily laps.

The doctors asked; "Tell me again what you did? What is your birth date?"

I told him 10/19/1940, He looked at me and started to smile. A few minutes later, I had the visit of a few more doctors and nurses; they all wanted to meet the 80 years old grandma, swimming 200 laps before coming to the ER. I insisted to tell them that it is a small pool, only 26 feet long.

To my surprise, Pastor Wes called me when I was in the ER that was during corona virus 19. No one was allowed to visit.

Pastor Wes   Pastor Keith   Charlene

Then Charlene also was on the phone to pray over me. I just imagined Abraham calling everybody to pray for me.

The test showed the bleeding was caused by the rupture of some cysts in my intestine. I had surgery to remove it, and IV antibiotic for 5 days.

During my stay, I was treated like a famous special person. A beautiful room in the new building. The first day, my assigned nurse came with a mask, like everybody during covid 19; I looked at her eyes and said to her;

"Do I know you?"

She took her mask off and said; "Yes Mrs. Michèle, I am Stephany, Pastor Keith's daughter."

I was amazed the way God surrounded me with people to care for me from the first day in the hospital. Can you only imagine the possibility in this huge hospital, in such a big medical facility, to have a nurse who normally works in a different unit to be especially assigned today to my room and to be the daughter to another loving caring pastor of the Church of God? that is not coincidence that is God watching over me. Yes! me a nobody according to the world, but a precious child of God according to my Lord.

Her father, pastor Keith, not young, a little heavy, but very active and very capable to fix things. When our dish washer broke down, I asked Pastor Keith if he could recommend someone from the church to repair it. Pastor Keith came himself he went down on his back on the floor.

I have never ever known any Pastor in my entire life that would do this. Lying on the floor at my feet! Fixing our dishwasher.

That day I realized that he was a living proof, of what Jesus said; "BY THIS ALL WILL KNOW THAT YOU ARE MY DISCIPLES IF YOU HAVE LOVE FOR ONE ANOTHER." (John 13:35)

When I asked him to pay for the new part and the work he did, Pastor Keith said everything was already taken care of.

WOW! That is really The Church of my Father God.

The insurance's medical worker wanted to meet me after listening to the hospital people gossiping about the 80 years old grandma with French accent swimming 200 laps.

I had the opportunity to ask her about her life, and to witness and pray over her the blessing of God. She came back with a bunch of papers with a social worker after I told her I would not go back to the hospital or see a doctor for a checkup because I did not want to pay the co-pay and that I needed to stay home since my husband had a very serious health problem.

The social worker said; "Starting today you and your husband will have free medical visitation and tests done at your home. And all your medication will be no more co-pay."

Praying for others and to be a witness turned out to be a huge blessing.

Every day I had the opportunity to be a witness and pray with someone, also with the Chaplain. Chaplains in hospitals, deal everyday with desperate people, everyone sucking the life out of the Chaplain, but they are just normal human beings like us, and need to be comforted just like me and you. He came in my room with a sad face and left with a smile.

Day four of my stay, I had a not so nice nurse, not because of her physical appearance but because of her bad attitude. She was a big black mama. She checked my vital signs...... my blood pressure was high.

She said; "You cannot have your medication until the doctor sees you because your pulse is under 60." She left.

The doctor came and said I should have the blood pressure medicine. She wrote it on the computer next to me, and another antibiotic IV. The doctor left and said the nurse needed to come immediately.

I rang for the nurse, 30 minutes later she was not here, I rang again... no nurse I rang the third time, and waited another 30 minutes. My blood pressure was getting worse. I became agitated, I pulled my IV out, and the other tubing I was tied to and got out of bed, opened the door and called out very loudly "NURSE!"

She was in the station talking and laughing with a male nurse. The doctors and students in the hallway were looking at me and her. She started to try to run in my direction.

She was mad, she pushed me in the room with her big breasts, closed the door and aggressed me verbally.

"I am not going to give you your medication, I don't take orders from patients because they lie!"

She was gesturing and moving her head like black people do when they argue.

Oh! She called me a liar? That really put fire in my brain.

I told her; "The doctor was here more than an hour ago, I ring 3 times, go look at the computer!"

I was so mad! That was war! But because she was such a "Big mama" I turned away and went in the shower.

Sitting under the hot water, trying to get my blood pressure to go down. I was not going to let her get away with that, she was wrong, and I am going to write a complaint against her.

Oh Lord please helps me! I started to talk to the Lord asking;

"Lord what is going on? Everything was so nice before this nurse came. Lord! Please tell me, I'm listening"

The Lord said; "YOU KNOW I GIVE YOU MY PEACE IN EVERY CIRCUMSTANCE, JUST LOOK AT ME, I DID IT ALL AT THE CROSS FOR YOU...................AND FOR HER"

I said; "Yes Lord"

The Lord said; "YOU KNOW I LOVE YOU............AND I LOVE HER."

I was in shock; "WHAT HER? EH LORD? Did you see what she did to me?"

The Lord let me have my introspection that was painful.
The question was my way or God's way?
The Lord let me to choose. OUCH my flesh was not willing.
After a little while, I got out of the shower and said; "All right Lord."

The nurse (let's call her Betty) asked me; "Are you OK Mrs. Ola?"

I went to the bed and told her to give me her hand, she said; "I don't hug!" I told her; "I don't want to hug you, just give me your hand."

She did, I closed my eyes and let the Holy Spirit to put the words in my mouth, I was willing to obey, but I needed help.

I prayed; "Lord blessed Betty...To be a nurse is not only a job but a ministry, to care for so many people, give her strength and favor in everything she does, and wherever she goes, I ask you Lord to put your angels around her, to keep her and her family safe, Amen."

I opened my eyes and saw tears in her eyes. Then everything changed she became so caring and nice for my last two days in the hospital.

Yes! Lord your way is always the best way.

LOVE HEALS!

Chapter 33

LIFE IS BEAUTIFUL WITH JESUS, FAMILY AND FRIENDS

Abraham was very curious to meet the owner of a new house who was just built on the main road, on the other side of our land.

We thought it must be a big family living there since the house was big and beautiful. Abraham put an invitation for the following Saturday's lunch in the mailbox. The owner came, he was a single man, his name was Peter, he was suspicious and not a happy man. He was worried about the corona virus and germs.

But we kept inviting him and he liked the fact, I had a French accent because his mother, who passed away a few years earlier, had a Polish accent. I asked him questions about Poland and he started to tell us about his story. He was in an orphanage in Poland and was adopted when he was 6 years old by an American doctor and his wife, whose background was also Polish.

Peter was over sixty years old he took his retirement as a Police Investigator. He decided to get away from the city. He was very reserved about his private life.

Slowly, after a few years, Peter became our most devoted best friend. Peter is now born again.

Peter has two German Shepherds, Duke a black 3 legged very friendly and smart, and Samson color tan is beautiful and obedient.

We are very close like family looking out for each other.

God is wonderful, he sent Peter near us to watch over us. Like a guardian angel in flesh. We live everyday thanking God for ALL He is providing for us to make our life easy.

I have to admit some days are more difficult. But the moment I surrender all to the Lord everything is good.

Today, Michelle, my close friend sent me a text with this; a Poster found in a church in France...(translated) THAT SAID;

"WHEN YOU ENTER THIS CHURCH IT MAY BE POSSIBLE THAT YOU HEAR THE CALL OF GOD! HOWEVER, IT IS UNLIKELY THAT HE WILL CALL YOU ON YOUR MOBILE. THANK YOU FOR TURNING OFF YOUR PHONES. IF YOU WANT TO TALK TO GOD, ENTER, CHOOSE A

QUIET PLACE AND TALK TO HIM. IF YOU WANT TO SEE GOD, SEND HIM A TEXT WHILE DRIVING."

Ha! ha! It is funny but so realistic; but people are still driving and texting.

I wanted so much to go see my younger daughter, Nouchka, who lives in Costa Rica. She was diagnosed with cancer in her throat.

During the rainy season, the roads where, so damaged with mudslides and potholes.

She had an accident as her car fell in a hole. Not only was the car damaged but also her foot, knee, her hip and her back. She never complained or asked me for anything. As a mother, I have her in my mind all the time and felt the urgency that she needed help.

I prayed Lord please send someone to be able to take care of Abraham for just a few days, for me to go pray over my daughter.

The next day Abraham got a very strange phone call from a black Bishop from New York.

He said he had an investigator to find his birth mother who gave him up for adoption when he was born. He discovered that his mother was white and she had passed away before he was able to meet her and his only relative alive is the cousin of his mother and that was Abraham. He wanted to meet Abraham and see pictures of his mother, she was brought-up with Abraham and his sister.

He came with his wife and his two daughters, to visit us.

He was very emotional and tears were pouring on his face, holding the pictures of his mother. They went back the same day. Then Cousin Kim called saying he would like to come and stay for a week to talk more with Abraham about his mother. I told him I would love to go to Costa Rica to visit my daughter. He said it would be an honor for him to take care of Abraham while I was away.

Glory to God! God answered his prayer and mine at the same time! What an AMAZING GOD we serve.

Pastor Wess prayed over me with the congregation and consecrated the oil that I was taking with me to anoint Nouchka.

When I arrived in Costa Rica, Nouchka was waiting for me with a smile. Her voice was weak and she was using a rod to walk. Her face was pale and she was in a lot of pain, but did not complain. I prayed over her, anointing her with oil.

When she was sleeping, I prayed in tongues and anointed the whole house. On the third day, Nouchka took her guitar and started to sing again, then in the evening she and me were dancing.

Halleluia! Praise the Lord! I stayed one week with her, loving every minute of it.

Back to the airport in San Jose, I met with a team of evangelists who were on a mission in Costa Rica, we became friends right away. I told them my story with Nouchka, showing them her dancing on my cell phone. The pastor leader, Franklin Culver (Church of the Holy Spirit), and his team stayed with me from Costa Rica to the Orlando airport helping me with my luggage.

A few months later, Franklin came to visit us in our farm.

He told Abraham; "Me and my team fell in love with your wife's powerful Godly Spirit in Costa Rica, and I would love to have her come to be a witness in our international convention in October."

Few days later, Abraham was in a lot of pain and needed to see a cardiologist immediately, instead driving 60 miles to Gainesville, we found a cardiologist who just opens a new office only 20 miles away.

We were delighted to meet Doctor Asad Qamar.

This man is a people person he can tell you what is wrong in your body and fix you only with just putting little devices in your body after a bunch of tests. Everyone who meets him, the first time, comes out of his office feeling they have a friend. He is really very different than any other doctors.

I am sure he is happy that all his clients are not like me.

Why? Because I witnessed to him, about my faith in Jesus, healing power in my life.

But Abraham and our dear friend Peter put their trust in men and were willing to have done all the procedures he told them was necessary for them to have. Doctor Qamar is so charming, that everyone who sees him cannot resist everything he says.

I like him. I really believe that Doctor Qamar has the gift of kindness, and my prayer over him is that one day he will ask Jesus to reveal himself to him, and be born again, and become a powerful winner of souls for the Kingdom of God.

We received a pleasant visit from Doug and Doylene, a wonderful couple from our church, bringing us lunch from a Japanese restaurant.

Doug and Doylene

They did not want me to have the trouble of cooking, and to give me a break, they brought the already prepared delicious food.

They both have such an amazing story of their life that it would take me a lot of pages to tell their story. They always have very lively, interesting conversations. They both served in the air force and then in the White House and the Pentagon, under 4 Presidents.

Doylene, this tiny incredible woman was an airplane mechanic for the President's Airforce one private jet.

Doug was in the intelligence service. He just told us something very interesting about the Vietnam war, that Abraham and I, did not know about.

"How Ho Chi Minh and his fellow Vietnamese nationalist, petitioned President Wilson when he came to France for the Versailles Peace Conference in 1919. They wanted help to get their freedom from France, but it was ignored.

Agents of the OSS, the Office of Strategic Services – the precursor to the CIA – were parachuted into the jungle of North Vietnam in early 1945 to make contact with him, in fact a US medic helped nurse him back to health from dysentery and malaria. The initial US intelligence assessment of Ho Chi Minh was more nationalist than communist and was an acceptable partner. The US provided him with weapons and training teams to help teach his guerrillas how to fight."

I must interact here...I cannot believe how stupide that was, training them to fight against us. Just like Biden giving the tax payer money to Iran to build nuclear weapons, to destroy Israel then America.

We must pray for America!

THOSE WHO TRUST IN THE LORD WILL RENEW THEIR STRENGTH THEY WILL SOAR ON WINGS LIKE EAGLES THEY WILL RUN AND NOT GROW WEARY THEY WILL WALK AND NOT FAINT. (Isaiah 40:31)

No one can understand God he is the creator. He is the potter and we are the clay.

"TO ERR IS HUMAN, TO FORGIVE IS DIVINE." (Alexander Pope 1711)

What an incredible Journey. We arrived in1984 in Florida, all our belongings stolen, no more money, no home, no relatives, no friends.

"BUT GOD! "When we trust Him, all things are possible. 40 years later in 2025 at 85 I have a wonderful live. My biggest miracle is to be able to see my children loving God!

"THE LORD IS MY SHEPHERD I SHALL NOT WANT. HE MAKES ME TO LIE DOWN IN GREEN PASTURES" Ps.23.

GOD IS FAITHFUL
The question is: ARE WE?

END

Note about accomplishments:

An interpreter businessman's in 2005: For Nigeria Ambassador and Pastors.

International Convention for "DEMOS RICHARD SHAKARIAN"

The United States of America

honors the memory of

RUSSELL HINMAN

This certificate is awarded by a grateful nation in recognition of devoted and selfless consecration to the service of our country in the Armed Forces of the United States.

Ronald Reagan

President of the United States

CHILDREN'S SERVICES COUNCIL
PALM BEACH COUNTY

THIS CERTIFICATE IS AWARDED TO

Michelle Ola

FOR COMPLETION OF THE WORKSHOP

Thoughts On Addiction

12/07/94

INSTRUCTORS:

Yvette Coursey, M.S.W., D.P.A.

Class Hours: 3
CEU's:

Trudy Hamor
Training & Development Associate
Children's Services Council

PROVIDER NUMBERS
NURSING: 27H0180
LCSW,LMFT,LMHC: CM-217-95

CHILDREN'S SERVICES COUNCIL
PALM BEACH COUNTY

THIS CERTIFICATE IS AWARDED TO

Michelle Ola

FOR COMPLETION OF THE WORKSHOP

Multiple Personality / Disorders In Adolescents

11/03/94

INSTRUCTORS:

Deborah Kidd McDonough, Psy.D.

Class Hours: 6
CEU's:

Trudy Hamor (signature)

Trudy Hamor
Training & Development Associate
Children's Services Council

PROVIDER NUMBERS
NURSING: 27H0180
LCSW.LMFT.LMHC: CM-217-95

CHILDREN'S SERVICES COUNCIL
PALM BEACH COUNTY

THIS CERTIFICATE IS AWARDED TO

Michelle Ola

FOR COMPLETION OF THE WORKSHOP

Post-Traumatic Stress In Children

11/10/94

INSTRUCTORS:

Mark Ellinger, Psy.D.

Class Hours: 5
CEU's:

Trudy Hamor
Training & Development Associate
Children's Services Council

PROVIDER NUMBERS
NURSING: 27H0180
LCSW,LMFT,LMHC: CM-217-95

247

CHILDREN'S SERVICES COUNCIL
PALM BEACH COUNTY

THIS CERTIFICATE IS AWARDED TO

Michelle Ola

FOR COMPLETION OF THE WORKSHOP

Children Of Addicted   Parents: Behavior Patterns

11/22/94

INSTRUCTORS:

Tony King, M.S., C.A.P., L.M.H.C.

Class Hours: 4
CEU's:

Trudy Hamor
Training & Development Associate
Children's Services Council

PROVIDER NUMBERS
NURSING: 27H0180
LCSW,LMFT,LMHC: CM-217-95

248

MICHELE OLA

From Europe to America
1983-2025

MIAMI BEACH - 1984

Me, Eric, and Nouchka in a
Cruise.

1987 WEDDING, WITH JEANNE ROTTENBURG

Eric, Nouchka, and
Pastor David

Earl with Nouchka

My 3 Children who are the light of my life and
help me to keep my eyes on Jesus Christ

Eric

Nouchka and Esther

Five generations intertwine—my mother, who came from France; me,
Nouchka; and Kira. Parents of George alongside Abraham, then followed by
his daughter Mimi and granddaughter Grace.

2003

In 2003, we moved to Morriston and built a 20-acre farm dedicated to caring for animals.

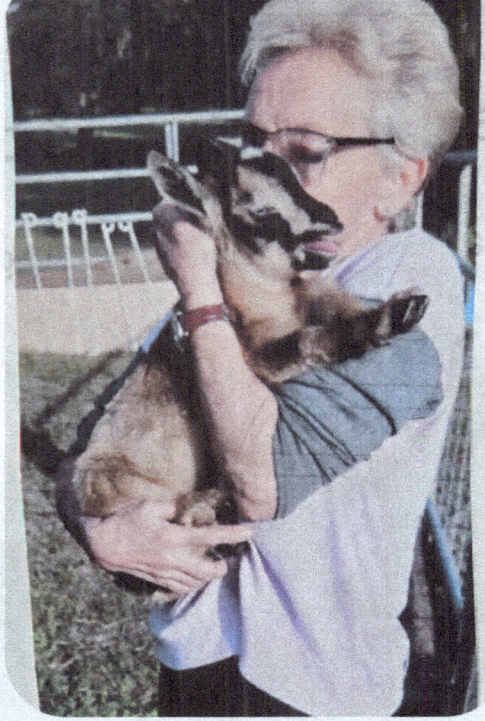

Morriston Farm

HORSE RIDING AT MORRISTON FARM

Teaching praise dancing, drama, and comedy, while Abraham focuses on educating students in school.

The Menninger Foundation and Boca Raton

Easter 2025 with my best friend Michelle

2025

Abraham

Me, Abraham, his daughter Jodi with Ana daughter-in-law

My Books

2011, ''BLOODY BAR KOCHBA''

2014, "REMEMBER"

2023, "IT ALL STARTS IN PARIS"

2023, "MAGIC CHRISTMAS"

2024, "GORGEOUS" (Abraham and Eric)

2025, "FROM THE SPOTLIGHT TO HIS GLORIOUS LIGHT"

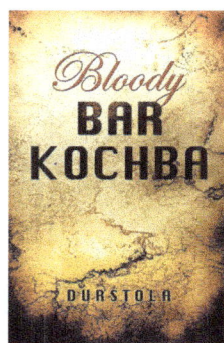

www.ingramcontent.com/pod-product-compliance
Lightning Source LLC
Chambersburg PA
CBHW080953120626
46546CB00010B/2881